Praise for *Slices of Community*

"I find my inspiration by connecting with the inspiring. In the last thirty years, I'm challenged to think of anyone as inspiring as Brad and Libby. The Birky's laid it ALL on the line in following their vision...and in succeeding...they've inspired tens of thousands. I'm just ONE of them."

— Shawn Anderson, Author, Speaker and Founder of Extra Mile America

"*Slices of Community* serves as a guide to give back, whether you walk away from the read to start your own unique community restaurant or you simply start to live in a way that views the people around you a little differently, with more compassion than before you cracked the book. The Birkys are the real deal: smart, funny, caring, no-nonsense people who recognize the strength in dignity, of community, of humanity. And they are masterful in the kitchen."

— Susan Hill Newton, Editor, University of Iowa Press

"A powerful manifestation of humanity, SAME Café solves the problem of food insecurity every day, by ordinary folks like you, me, and the stranger on the street. Step inside this inception story, illuminating a hopeful path that begins with healthy, delicious food for ALL. Discover the impact that comes with serving up dignity alongside a slice of pizza and a side salad. Meet some of the folks who shaped the café's early years, and encounter a rare community of misfits, creatives,

volunteers, friends and neighbors. Dream about more profoundly different places like SAME Café."

— Mary Hambrick, Volunteer, Activist, Mother, and Expert in Food Justice

SLICES OF COMMUNITY

STORIES FROM BEHIND THE COUNTER OF THE COUNTRY'S OLDEST PAY-WHAT-YOU-CAN RESTAURANT

Brad Birky

Published in the United States by:
BLInc Publishing, Englewood, FL

Text copyright ©2022 Brad Birky

Edited by Ignited Press, Littleton, CO
Cover artwork by Alaina Kornfeld, Chicago, IL

First printed October 2022

ISBN: 979-8-9871258-2-3

Authors' Note

This book has been a collaborative process even though there is only one name on the cover. I thought I would take a minute to introduce myself and share with you how this book came to be in existence. You'll see this book is written from Brad's perspective, but we worked on every line together. My name is Libby Birky and I am Brad's wife.

We wrote this book because we wanted to share stories of the café to make sure we weren't the only ones who knew the magic that happens in that place. Most of our customers struggled daily, not just to put healthy food on their plates but to find connection. Even on the hardest of days, the pure love and light shared in that space was amazing. We have seen some of the most inspiring moments in spite of the struggle.

I think SAME Café and many of the other community cafés that exist are a handbook on being human. They are places where people are accepted for who they are and where they are in life, and in turn accept others. We wanted to share these stories with you to illustrate what a beautiful place SAME Café is and to document them so we won't forget their impact on us.

We drew on our own memories as well as our interviews with customers, friends, and volunteers. We also dug deep into the archives of the printed articles about SAME and sometimes even included portions from people in their own words when we couldn't figure out how to say it any better.

Throughout the book you'll find photographs and some published writings from our newsletters and blogs. When we could, we gave credit where credit was due. If not specifically cited, the photos were taken by one of us. Also, we changed a few names along the way to protect individual privacy.

There is a section of this book for every reader. If you want to understand how to build community in a unique restaurant setting, there is a part of this book for you. Maybe you are reading this because you have been to SAME Café and were curious if the cookie recipe was included; sorry, we cannot help you there. Maybe you picked up this book because you have heard about SAME Café (or one of the many other community cafés that are open around the country) but have never been in. We are so glad you are reading our book and we hope that after you finish you will visit one of the cafés and experience the magic for yourself.

But really this book is about people, connection, hope and community. We tried to include as much of the history of SAME Café as we could while keeping the heart of this book about inspiring people we met along the way. We consider many of them to be our heroes. A hero gives something up for the good of others. Some of these heroes were experiencing homelessness while others had homes that were big enough to host 100+ people parties. I think most people will agree that the true mark of a hero is sacrifice, and every one of the people you'll read about made sacrifices to help others. These stories hopefully cause you to change in some way after you have read them. Maybe you open your heart just a little more to a neighbor in need. Maybe you start seeing that guy flying a sign on the corner as a human being who could use a smile. We hope these stories can reach beyond the page and touch you the way they have touched us.

SAME Café is an extraordinary place, but as one of our long-time supporters reiterated to us, it is the people who make the place. SAME Café would not exist today without the heroes who dined there, volunteered there, donated to the cause, or even just spread the word. SAME Café is dedicated to making healthy food available to anyone who walks through the door, regardless of ability to pay. What really happens there is that people are seen, heard, and valued. They feel safe and comfortable speaking up, listening, respecting one another, helping and sacrificing for each other every day. It is a place where inherent dignity is affirmed and shared. What can you sacrifice today for the good of others?

Prologue

As I hand the plate across the counter into the familiar hands of the customer who ordered it, I can't help but smile. I watch as Aussie John takes the plate—filled to the brim with whole wheat pizza, spring greens with cranberries and bleu cheese, and a cup of potato leek soup—and walks away without paying. I smile because I know after he finishes eating, John will gladly put on an apron and wash dishes for at least an hour to pay for his meal.

Working for a meal at SAME Café is the only way John can afford to eat healthy foods. Dozens of others who come through the café doors every day are in the same situation. Fresh, whole foods like those served at SAME Café are almost always too expensive. They also aren't sold anywhere close to the neighborhoods where the poorest Americans live. In most areas of this country, the foods that are the most affordable are highly processed and nutrient deficient. This readily available "food" is cause for so many of today's health problems—including diabetes and heart disease.

The faces of hunger can vary greatly, and they are not necessarily what people might think. There are those that many of us think of first: the homeless men and women we see panhandling on street corners or lying on blankets under bushes in the park. But then there are the approximately 775,000 individuals in Colorado alone who are far less visible, yet equally as vulnerable: the food insecure. These are neighbors, co-workers, relatives, and friendly acquaintances who do not know where their next meal might be coming from, if at all. These are single parents who are struggling to work enough hours to put food on the table while paying for childcare. They are elderly people on fixed incomes who are being buried by medical expenses and the general costs of aging. They are also students, artists and musicians who live on next to no income, surviving on dried noodles and cereal.

In 2006, the *Denver Post* reported that the number of Colorado households struggling to put a meal on the table had risen nearly 3% since 2003. According to the City and County of Denver's Food Vision 2017, 33.2% of Denver families eat less than one serving of fruits and vegetables per day.

This lack of access to proper foods, along with lack of choice and the distinct absence of dignity are among the chief reasons that SAME Café was created. It was important to us that customers were able to have some control over their lunch choice, so we decided to offer two choices in each category. The ingredients were going to be sourced locally, sustainably and organically whenever possible. At least one choice in each category was going to be vegetarian, not only to appeal to a wider range of diners, but also to keep our costs down. SAME Café was created to address food insecurity, but it became so much more than that. It became a space where community was built and connections were made, all over plates of pizza, salad and cookies.

Chapter 1

It All Started with an Idea

The conversation had started like most of them had in the past, but this time something was different. We were flying back to Denver after a trip to Austin when the inspiration hit us. You often hear about people experiencing an "Aha" moment, but up until this point, we hadn't experienced anything like that. This time was different. We could both feel the excitement bubbling inside of us as we discussed our idea. This seemed crazy but it could actually work!

Libby grabbed the in-flight magazine from the seat in front of her and flipped open to a page with some white space so we could take notes. I scribbled down the ideas as fast as they came out of our mouths.

"Let's call it Dine and Dash!" I suggested, thinking that it could be a cute way to integrate cooking and running, which were two of my passions.

"Um no, I don't think that's the message we want to send," Libby replied. "I think it should have white table clothes and servers. It needs to beautiful inside."

"I love making breakfast foods, maybe we should serve breakfast?"

Libby responded, "Um no again. Breakfast places have to open up by 6 am. I refuse to get up that early. Plus the food needs to be healthy—how are you going to make bacon and eggs healthy?"

Ok, so not every thought that came out of the brainstorming session was a winner. But one thing seemed certain, the universe was telling us we needed to open a new kind of restaurant. A restaurant that served healthy food but had no set prices. A restaurant where no one would be turned away because they didn't have enough money to buy a meal.

Some of the other nuggets that we wrote down that day were pure gold, and would become the basis for how it would work:

- Pay what you can afford
- Staffed by volunteers/homeless
- Partner with other local organizations
- Offer nutrition/cooking classes
- Learn people's names
- Invite visiting/guest chefs to cook
- Everyone is welcome as long as you are polite
- Serve great coffee and great food to great people

The year was 2002, and an idea was starting to take root. Were we crazy? Maybe. But we knew one thing from our previous volunteering experiences. People were being treated like they WERE less because they HAD less. We knew there had to be another way.

But I'm getting ahead of myself a little. Let's back up and find out how we started to have this conversation in the first place.

When I graduated in 1993 from high school in rural midwestern Illinois, I could have never imagined being a chef or starting a restaurant. Towards the end of high school, my family finally got a home computer, and I immediately took it apart to learn how it worked. I even managed to correctly put it back together. Computers fascinated me, and I knew that's what I wanted to study in college. The thought of cooking in a restaurant couldn't have been further from my mind.

Four years later, I found myself with a computer science degree from a reputable engineering school. Upon graduation, I immediately married my long-distance girlfriend, Libby Whalen. The two of us quickly found work—Libby as an elementary school teacher and I as a computer consultant. The jobs were fine—neither of us worked horrible hours and we were able to spend time together in the evenings and weekends. The pay was good enough that we could afford to occasionally take a trip or dine at a nice restaurant.

We lived on the edge of a tiny town with a population of 2,000 just outside of Peoria, Illinois. By "tiny," I mean there wasn't even a single stop light. It was an agricultural area, filled with both farmers and the businesses who supported them. Right across the street from our small, two-bedroom house was a huge field that grew commodity crops, alternating between soybeans and field corn each year. Both of our families were less than a thirty minute drive away, still living in the communities where we had spent our childhoods.

Growing up in the Midwest, Libby and I had very similar upbringings. We are both middle children and our parents had similar careers. Our dads were both in construction, and our moms worked in schools. Both of our families were active in their churches. Although I was raised Mennonite and Libby was raised Catholic, even going to Catholic school all the way through college, we were both used to volunteering. I can remember singing carols at the local home for seniors and going on church mission trips to work on houses. Libby's family volunteered regularly with Special Olympics and a local food pantry. She also has lots of memories of standing outside grocery stores with her sisters, raising funds for local charities while eating the Tootsie Rolls they were supposed to be handing out to donors.

We also had memories of growing up with delicious food from both professional and home kitchens. Libby's mother had worked at the public high school in the cafeteria. She remembers some days when her mom would have to take Libby and her sisters to work with her in the early mornings. She can still remember the huge industrial mixing bowl her mom would use to combine ingredients for the school day's desserts that were made by hand. She loved those days because she got to sample the dessert and have chocolate milk for breakfast. To this day, when she smells a snickerdoodle cookie, it takes her right back to that high school kitchen. One of her favorite at-home meal memories was going to the garden that was on the lot right next door her house to harvest ripe zucchini. The zucchini slices were then breaded in cracker crumbs and fried in an electric skillet that rested on top of the washing machine in the family kitchen.

For years, my maternal grandparents owned a small bar/restaurant in the same tiny town where Libby and I lived in the first few years of marriage. My Uncle Frank was the main cook, and Grandma Swearingen would pay my mom to deep clean the restaurant every Friday before the weekend's fried chicken dinner special. I remember the interior of the place smelling like whiskey and cigarettes. My brother, sister, and I would often come along and try to be "helpful" while Mom cleaned. If we were good and not too much of a bother to the regulars who held court at the bar, Grandma would let us have a Ginger Ale or a "Kiddie Cocktail" as payment for our services.

On Sundays, we would often get together for dinner at my other grandparents' house. Grandma Birky would serve up platters of roast beef, mashed potatoes, and the ever-present Jello salad (we lovingly call it Pink Fluff). Everyone in the family who could make the dinner would crowd around the table in their small living room. People would catch up on family news as we ate our fill. It really didn't matter what we were eating, what I remember most is the time we spent together and the relationship building that went on during these dinners.

The consulting company I worked for out of college gave us the option of taking additional paid days to do volunteer work. That option was a no-brainer for us. Even as a dating couple we had made a point to continue to volunteer with organizations we felt strongly about. Many conversations throughout our dating and early married life were about our plans for the future. We seriously considered doing some sort of Peace Corp or other mission work. Even though we felt deep down we had a calling for service, we just couldn't quite pull the trigger and commit to any full-time program. When we found out about this option with my job, we jumped at the opportunity. We called and scheduled some volunteer shifts in the kitchen of the local mission. We were quickly hooked.

Once the handful of paid days from my company were used up for the year, we didn't want the volunteering to end. We signed up for a regular Tuesday night shift. Besides the two of us, we worked with a recently retired couple from the area who would sometimes bring along another friend. There were also a couple of guys on hand to help who stayed at the mission. They had been around for a while and were in the beginning stages of a combination addiction rehabilitation and job readiness program. On average, the mission fed and housed eighty to ninety men a night.

Every Tuesday we would show up an hour or so before dinner, and Don, the kitchen manager, would give us our assignments. Some nights we would peel potatoes and carrots, other nights we might be in charge of mixing the powdered drink du jour. One of the most memorable nights was being set up in the corner of the kitchen with a small coffee grinder and about fifty small bags of donated coffee beans, grinding batch after batch so they could have plenty of ground coffee on hand for the breakfast shift. This weekly stint continued on Tuesday nights for nearly four years. We even had matching t-shirts embroidered with "Tuesday Night Mission Crew" for all of us.

Some days we worked to create something filling and edible out of canned and boxed foods. At times there were donations of produce and meats that could be worked with as well. These "fresh" items were always tricky—for every tray of good strawberries donated, there were ten that had grown so moldy that they looked like the berries wore fur coats. The volunteer crew dutifully picked through them until only the passable few remained to be added to the dinner trays, and we trashed the rest. Other days, we would sort through garbage bags filled with brown, oozing lettuce in an attempt to make a salad. It still looked inedible even when smothered with ranch dressing. It was on days like this when Libby and I would look sadly at the meal that we had helped to create and silently agree we would pick something up to eat on the way home. Luckily for us, we had the luxury of making that choice. Choice wasn't available to the residents—they either ate the meal that was offered or they went without.

The only interaction we had with the mission residents, other than the few we worked with in the kitchen, was handing them plastic trays of food through the service window. If the volunteers chose to eat at all, they and mission staff ate at a separate table after the men were served. The men ate quickly and quietly, then bussed their own trays and headed to the chapel in neat, orderly rows. More often than not, we would head home right after dinner, having barely talked to any of the residents staying at the shelter. We knew next to nothing about these guys, many of whom we saw once a week for four years. There was rarely a chance to learn someone's name let alone build a relationship with them. This lack of interaction really bothered us both, as it seemed to foster an "us and them" dynamic that just didn't feel right.

It also seemed weird to us that guests were required to attend a church service. We were free to stay for the service if we liked, and occasionally we did. The more we volunteered and stayed for the church service, the more it bothered us that church was a mandatory part. The men clearly weren't interested in attending; many of them slept in the pews or read books during the service.

We loved our volunteering time at the mission, and the good feeling we got from knowing we were helping feed the guys who stayed there. After our time at the mission came to a close, the many hours we spent volunteering there had a long-lasting impact on the two of us.

The Dot Com bubble had recently burst, and by early 2002 the repercussions had finally wormed their way into central Illinois. As a computer consultant, we knew I was on borrowed time. Libby had recently graduated with a master's degree in curriculum and instruction with an emphasis on gifted education. In our area, these types of jobs were few and far between. All signs were pointing to relocation in order to find the type of work we desired. Once my layoff was official, that sealed the deal.

We narrowed the short list of prospective cities down to Kansas City, Austin, and Denver and let the resumes fly. As expected, I had next to no response from my inquiries. Luckily it was only a matter of weeks before a school in Denver showed interest in Libby. She flew out for the interview and was offered the job. We decided to take that as a sign that Denver was our kind of town.

Don was a middle-aged New England transplant who struggled with alcoholism, which caused him to be on the streets. Staying at the mission and proving himself through the sobriety program led him to the job of kitchen manager. He hoped to gain enough experience in the kitchen to open his own place someday. Don's job was to make up meals from whatever staple items he had on hand along with any "fresh" items that had been donated that day.

I can remember clearly being asked to make creamed peas once. Being newly married and not having any expertise in the kitchen just yet, neither of us had any idea how to make creamed peas from scratch. But Don just pointed us in the direction of the huge tilting skillet and in his thick Boston accent said, "Have at it!"

"You've got to be kidding me," Libby said to me once Don walked away. "What are we supposed to do with these?" She held up a huge can of peas. It didn't help that Libby hated eating creamed peas. It was the texture that freaked her out the most. I grabbed the bag of flour to see if there was a recipe on the back, but no luck. We were clueless. We dumped the peas, flour, and some milk into the skillet and crossed our fingers. It was a bit of a disaster to say the least, and what we created could only be described as looking like wallpaper paste. I couldn't even get Libby to taste it, which is probably good because it didn't taste any better than it looked. But it was served anyway. We looked at each other in shame as we saw each scoop of the stuff being dropped onto serving trays.

We learned quite a bit from Don over the years. He was adept at coming up with dishes on the fly.

With one look into the pantry, he could construct an entire night's meal. It was like watching a low budget version of the show *Iron Chef* as he pulled out ingredients and invented new dishes. Don also taught us a few tricks. One is that salt is absorbent. We found that out when Libby drained the fryer to clean it and the hot oil melted through the container she used. The oil went all over the kitchen floor! Don opened a big bag of salt and spread it over the spill. Then, we just swept it up with a broom. It was much easier than wiping up oil.

Chapter 2

Heading West

Things just flew from that point forward. Our house hit the market and sold in less than a month. On a weekend trip, I found an apartment near downtown Denver to rent and signed the lease without ever seeing the inside. (Luckily it turned out to be a great space!) Two weeks later we drove back with all our possessions in a moving van.

We had originally thought we would have a couple of months to get used to the city together before Libby had to report to her new school for work. Even that got short-tracked when I got a call out of the blue to interview for a temporary IT consulting job with a downtown law firm. I reported to work less than two weeks after we made it into town.

Before long, we felt the tug to fill the volunteer void in our lives. There was something about volunteering that nourished us. Through each of our volunteer experiences, we learned something about humanity. The connections that we made with the people we met, either those we were serving or serving with, were profound.

Each time we volunteered, we felt we got more than we gave. Over and over again, when we took the time to get to know people, we were reminded that people are people no matter their struggles in life.

We had recently reconnected with a college friend of Libby's who, along with her partner, was doing some volunteer work at the Denver Catholic Worker House. "The Worker," as it was known to the residents and volunteers, was a two-story house in downtown Denver. It provided more than just meals and resources; it was a home. The individuals and families staying there were trying to find work, save for an apartment, make connections and get back on their feet. We were invited to come to The Worker for a couple of shifts, and once again we were in the volunteer groove.

Each week we would show up, cook dinner for the twelve to fifteen residents and live-in workers, and then we would sit down at the large dining table and eat the meal together. After dinner, we would stick around for a few hours so the others could take an evening off. We would watch movies, play games, or just hang out with the residents. This combination of cooking, dining together, and building community was amazing. It was becoming apparent that volunteering once a week wasn't quite enough anymore.

The temp job at the law firm continued month to month. While it showed no signs of ending anytime soon, we knew there was always the possibility it wouldn't get renewed, and I would once again be looking for work. This instability was cause for many more discussions about what we eventually wanted our future to look like. For us it was important that a job would provide a sense of fulfillment as well as a paycheck.

Our friends from the Catholic Worker were feeling like they were in a similar transitional phase, so the four of us met for hours to talk about the possibilities. While we were new in town as well as relatively new to volunteering in Denver, they had contacts with several groups in Denver's non-profit world. Several of the meetings also included Sister Anna, who had founded The Worker twenty-five years earlier and had extensive contacts in local service organizations.

Anna's advice was if we couldn't find an organization that felt right or seemed to do what we thought needed to be done, maybe we should create one ourselves. This wisdom really sunk in and changed the direction of our discussions from trying to find a group where we fit in to doing quite a bit of introspection and trying to identify what would actually be helpful. We wanted to walk alongside people.

We stopped thinking about which organization could help and started thinking about what it was that we wanted to do. Lots of existing organizations focused on food access but not on what they were providing or how it was being provided. It seemed they cared more about the numbers they served and the pounds of food distributed than the people and how they were being treated. Let alone, what they were putting into their bodies. Boxed noodles and canned vegetables were not what we had in mind, nor was making people fill out forms and stand in long lines. It seemed like the current system was lacking in so many ways. We were excited about getting good, healthy food into the hands of those who couldn't afford it and thought it needed to be done in a dignified way.

Just what to do with our feelings and ideas escaped us until that flight, but then it hit us, and everything made perfect sense. We could open a restaurant! People often ask us where the idea came from. I joke that maybe it was the lack of oxygen from flying at 30,000 feet, at which point Libby chimes in, "Or maybe it was because we were closer to God?" No matter where it came from, once the idea was in our heads, we knew we had to make it a reality.

When the flight landed back in Denver, we started to think things through a little more. We quickly realized that a few of our ideas just weren't feasible. The name "Dine and Dash" wouldn't get the right message across, so we threw that aside. Making breakfast would mean waking up at 5am or earlier every workday. Neither of us was willing to make that commitment just yet, especially when we could just as easily serve lunch and/or dinner instead. We had no idea if we could let people "pay" for their meal by volunteering. We were definitely going to have to do some research.

After talking to the volunteers and residents of The Worker, we made what was possibly the most important adjustment so far. We decided to pursue a casual café style setup rather than the formal one we had originally pictured. The feedback we got from the residents we spoke with was that they would feel so unwelcome and out of place in a white tablecloth restaurant atmosphere that they wouldn't even bother walking in the door. Societal rules have told them for so long that only those who play the part, those with lots of money who are well dressed, can enter and eat at those establishments. The idea of a casual café seemed much more approachable and welcoming to people of all income levels. It never dawned on us until that point that someone wouldn't feel comfortable walking into a fancy restaurant space. It was a huge lesson for us on how important it was to step inside someone else's shoes and really listen rather than assume we know what is best for others.

The two of us were totally excited about a restaurant, even if we had no idea how to build such a venture. We had some good feedback from the folks at The Worker, but how would friends and family take this crazy plan? The close friends that we initially shared our ideas with were very supportive, but unsure of how successful a restaurant like that could really be.

One of our closest friends asked us a key question that really cemented our faith in the idea. "What happens if the restaurant fails?" This was the first time we had been asked this, and the answer that we came back with became a major motivator in the startup process. We quickly answered, "The restaurant can't fail.

As long as we manage to open and feed one person that needs a meal, then it will have been a success." That thought would keep us going in the coming months when roadblocks to opening would pop up and try to derail our progress.

Our parents were cautiously optimistic about our plans. They loved the concept and wanted to help in any way possible. But they also wanted to make sure their kids were also thinking about the long term. They asked many of the tough questions for which we had no answers.

- How would we pay our bills?
- Would we keep our other jobs?
- Would we have health insurance in case something catastrophic happens?
- And maybe the biggest question of the moment —Where would we get the money to start?

While we didn't have the answers quite yet—we weren't going to let that stop us. This idea was so strong and our passion to make it happen was so deep, we knew the details would work themselves out. What we did know was that we could cook. Thanks to our years of volunteering at the mission and The Worker, we had lots of practice. What we didn't know yet was how much we were about to be challenged and changed.

It was 2005 before we were ready to start making some real progress towards opening a restaurant. We both loved to cook, but since neither of us had any formal training, we decided that one of us needed to enroll in a culinary program. The only problem was we both wanted to go. However, since I had the more flexible job situation, we decided (after a couple of tough games of rock paper scissors) that I would take the classes. After looking at a couple of different options for schools, we found one program that was affordable and flexible enough.

I was able to keep working part time at my day job and take classes in the afternoons and evenings. The Metropolitan State University campus was close enough to downtown that I could bike back and forth between class and the office. In the evenings that I didn't have class, we would have our own culinary school of sorts in our home kitchen where I would teach Libby the skills I was learning that week. One of her favorite memories from these early days was making caramelized onion gruyere tarts from scratch and roasting olives with orange zest and rosemary.

Culinary school was great. Not only did I learn some knife skills and insights into what flavors paired well together, but I also gained some much-needed kitchen confidence. Thanks to those lessons, we would be able to turn out a consistent and high-quality product that would attract diners from all income brackets. It didn't hurt that we got to eat really good food! Up until that point, our evening meals often consisted of grilled cheese sandwiches or casseroles. It felt good to expand our palates and learn a host of new recipes.

It was also in that year that we found a restaurant in Salt Lake City which operated something like what we were hoping to create called One World Café. We had been scouring the internet, but until this point, we were unable to find anything in the US close to what we were dreaming. The One World founder, Denise Cerreta, was a former acupuncturist turned restaurateur who had the vision of ending world hunger while promoting organic foods and healthy eating. We planned a trip for that summer to go to Utah, see some national parks, and visit and volunteer at One World. We had never been to Salt Lake City before, but we found the café easily enough because it was right near the tabernacle at the center of the city.

We did not alert them to our coming ahead of time. We wanted to experience the café just as any customer would experience it. As we walked in the door, we knew right away that some of our restaurant design would be inspired by what they had in place. The kitchen area was completely open, making it possible for kitchen staff and volunteers to easily communicate and interact with customers. A donation box in the form of a treasure chest was available on the counter for diners to insert their meal payment, and change was available if needed from one of the staff. If someone didn't have cash to pay but wanted to earn a meal, there was a sign-up board where they could volunteer for an hour instead. The menu was a rotating variety of salads, soups and quiche prepared in house with a very minimal amount of equipment. While we ate lunch, we took good notes of all the things about their set up we liked as well as what we might need or want to do differently.

One World Café had been set up inside the space where Denise had previously had her acupuncture practice. Their kitchen was open, but extremely crowded and dark. The dining areas were several small appointment rooms, each with its own unique decorative theme. We found that eclectic and fun but saw how it could be challenging for community building and meaningful interactions. On their donation box was posted a suggested donation range of $8-$18 for a meal, although folks could drop whatever they liked into the box (or of course take the volunteer option). We loved the idea of an anonymous donation box and knew we would work that into our setup somehow.

There was also the option to have the free item which was available out of a soup kettle in a corner of the café self-service style. It was often a staple hearty dish. The first day we were there it was rice and beans. The second day it was lentils.

After lunch we signed up to volunteer the next day and asked if Denise was around. She happened to live above the café, and we were told she was on her way down. We wanted to set up a meeting with Denise to talk about our plans for a Denver café. She was more than happy to tell us about her experiences and offer some great advice right then and there. We sat in the café and talked for a long while. Some of her key points were start small, be consistent, find a great board of directors, pay cash for everything, and be easy to find. She even offered to come to Denver whenever we got a space to help us get it ready to open.

Back in our room at a local motel, we couldn't stop talking. Our visit was rehashed through hours of conversation. We talked about the food options and what we ate. A lot of the conversation revolved around how awesome it was that Denise was so open and helpful to us. Going to bed that night, we were exhausted but excited to volunteer and see what it was all about.

Salt Lake City, and all of Utah, had a food-handlers permit requirement, which meant patrons had a hard time volunteering in their kitchen. Most of the volunteer opportunities were cleaning the dining areas or outside in their garden. Since I was attending culinary school and knew all the requirements, we were allowed to help in the kitchen. Arriving early in the morning, we were put right to work peeling vegetables. For the first time in a commercial space, we saw the saving of vegetable peels and ends to make stock. I had made stock in culinary school this way and was excited to see them making stock from scratch. This would be something we would do in our space.

Libby and I watched everything carefully happen over our volunteer day. The space was limited but they were able to do a ton with it. This really opened our eyes to the possibilities. Up until this point, we had envisioned a fully functioning restaurant kitchen and knew that would be our biggest hurdle because of the expense. This kitchen consisted of two soup pots, a conveyor style mini oven, a large reach in fridge, and a sink. It was basic but fully functional.

One of our most profound moments with Denise was when she said, "You can always go back to your old life." For whatever reason, this idea felt like do or die to us. The notion that we could go back to teaching or computer science jobs had never really seemed an option until that moment. It was like a light bulb went off in our heads. It gave us the confidence we needed to take the leap. Like she said, we could always go back.

While we were there, our unopened and conceptual café got its first bit of press. Denise had an interview scheduled with the local newspaper, *The Deseret News*. She invited us to sit with them and chat with the author about our idea. Up to this point, One World Café was an anomaly. The author was excited to include the idea was growing, potentially in Denver.

As we drove out of Salt Lake City to make the return trip to Denver, our minds were spinning. We were so focused on making plans and talking about everything we had just experienced, we barely noticed the incredible scenery we were driving through. Now that we had finally seen an example of a pay-what-you-can restaurant, we had no doubt it was going to be possible for us to create one of our own. Even if it wasn't set up exactly like ours was planned to be, we now had something concrete to which we could refer.

On the way back we talked a lot about the payment system. The suggested donation range seemed to say $8 was the minimum. We could pay $8 per person but we asked each other, "What if we didn't have $16?" It felt uncomfortable immediately. We wondered how other people would feel. Would that cause some people to not return because they felt they didn't have enough to offer? And what about someone who wanted to help pay it forward? If they saw the $8-$18 range, would they give more than the $18? Something just didn't feel right.

We were also adamant that everyone should order off the same menu whether they were donating money or time. We thought an important part of this idea was everyone should have access to the same high-quality food. We felt strongly that we wanted to make our café work this way, to be inclusive and treat everyone the same.

Our visit to Salt Lake really created more questions than answers for us and we started to get nervous. Would a restaurant where anyone could eat really work? Would we be seen as the white saviors swooping in to help poor people? We wondered if people would really build connections? Would people be generous with their time and money in ways that could make it work? Not just rich white church ladies, but would everyone come to the café? Would it really be a place of connection? Was connection enough? We knew from personal experience connecting to others was what brought us back time and time again to volunteering. It was what made a difference for us. It filled our cups and made us whole. Connection to a community was what we were missing. We assumed others were missing that too.

Sister Anna had overcome so many obstacles in her life, both as a Denver Catholic Worker founder and as an advocate for peace and justice. She started The Worker in the late 1970s in the model of an activist named Dorothy Day, who set the precedent for walking alongside those in poverty. Anna was not afraid to speak up when she saw an injustice and frequently protested against organizations that promote violence.

The Denver Catholic Worker became a place where those who were homeless and struggling could not only get food and shelter, but also regain a sense of dignity. The residents of the house can use The Worker phone number and address on resumes and job applications. This made it easier for potential employers to reach them, as well as gave the residents the feeling that they belonged somewhere instead of being shuffled from shelter to shelter. The phone at The Worker was always answered with a simple

"Hello," because it was a residence and not a social service agency.

The Worker was much more a home than most, and we loved the feel of the place. Being around people like Anna encouraged us to follow our hearts and our passions.

Chapter 3

Moving Forward

One significant question kept coming up as we told more people about our idea. "How are you going to fund this?" We were so naïve that neither of us worried too much about it. It wasn't until we got a mentor from the Small Business Administration when reality started to sink in. He actually laughed when I shared our idea with him. By that point, we had a flimsy business plan with projections and estimates (that were way off in retrospect). Our mentor brought to our attention that most new restaurants fail within a year. Of those that make it beyond their first anniversary, 59% fail within three years. No bank would be interested in loaning any money to a couple with zero experience in the culinary industry and very little collateral.

This shocked us and made us begin to realize all those people who were wondering about money were probably on the right track. We should have had a better plan by this point for finances. But we aren't really money people—we are doers. So, we decided to just keep doing and hope things would fall into place.

As we started scouring the city for properties that could work, we started to realize we needed funds sooner rather than later. We added up our net worth and tried to figure out how much money we could scrape together. While we weren't swimming in money, we were frugal people. We didn't have kids and we had two decent incomes. We had a little bit in savings, plus our retirement funds in the form of IRAs and 401Ks.

Our parents were less than excited that we were considering taking all the money out of our retirement accounts. Everything they learned about finance told them once that money is invested, you should never touch it until you reach retirement age. We weren't thinking or worried about retirement. Our singular focus was getting this restaurant open by any means possible. We were more concerned with getting to our retirement years and looking back and asking, "What if?" What if we had invested in community? What if we had started that restaurant we always talked about? We didn't want to have any regrets around this idea. In our gut, we knew cafés like these needed to exist, and they would work. If no one was going to loan us money, then we would loan the restaurant what startup capital we could pull together.

We started going through the motions of filling out the necessary withdrawal forms to gather our life savings into a neat little stack, and the total of the loan came out to $24,000. It seemed like a measly pile when you think about the amount of money it normally takes to open a restaurant. Our stockpile turned out to be one third of what was recommended by everyone we spoke to in the industry.

In the meantime, we had finally come up with a name for our concept—SAME Café. SAME was an acronym that stood for **S**o **A**ll **M**ay **E**at, but it also had the double meaning that all customers would be treated equally. The inspiration for the name came from Libby's volunteer experience in college. She had gone with a group of students to Washington, D.C. to volunteer at the D.C. Central Kitchen. While in D.C., she volunteered with a program called SOME – **S**o **O**thers **M**ight **E**at. Our café name was an homage to Libby's experience there and the impact it had on her. Throughout these months we were recording our progress (or lack of it) on a free blog site so our family and friends could keep informed. When it came to naming the café, we put out a post with several options and asked people to vote for their favorite. SAME Café was the top pick by far. Other favorite options were Earl's (after Libby's grandpa) and Simon's (after my grandpa).

Since we were trying to open the restaurant with the bare minimum of funds, we turned to the old school style of raising money. We sent out a physical letter to friends and family asking them to sponsor items we would need to make SAME Café happen. Libby remembers the day when our first pizza cutter and pan arrived from some of our greatest friends in Madison, Wisconsin. SAME Café still has that cutter today! We also got shipments of spatulas, bread pans and aprons. My grandma even sent us a check for enough money to buy a refrigerator. We did crowdfunding before crowdfunding was a thing.

This is the actual list of what we asked people to sponsor or get for us. The response to that letter was amazing. It was like Christmas each time a package arrived. With our meager life savings of $24,000 and the $6,000 in supplies and donations from this crowdfunding campaign wish list, we moved forward with confidence. Like in a game of poker, we were going all in and betting on community.

Item	Quantity Needed	Approximate Cost (each)
Nugget Ice Machine	1	$5,000
Refrigerator	1	$3,000
Freezer	1	$1,000
Stainless Steel Tables	2	$200
Large Pots	5	$80
Large Fry Pans	5	$35
Baking Dishes	3	$35
Food Processor	1	$750
Plastic Tubs for Storage — Square, various sizes	20	$10
Shelves/Racks	5	$330
Blender	1	$170
Water Pitchers	10	$10
Salt and Pepper Shakers	12	$5
Napkin Dispensers	12	$30
Plates, silverware, glasses	0	Already purchased ☺
Pizza Trays	4	$5
Pizza Knife	1	$45
Plastic Spatulas	5	$5
Baking Sheets	5	$20
Sheet Pans	5	$15
Ingredient Bins	3	$185
Soup Warmer	2	$200
Knives	10	$50
Cutting Board Set	1	$120
China Cap Strainer	2	$20
Tongs	2	$2
Can Opener	1	$165
Mixing Bowl Set	2	$50
Bistro Chairs	20	$100
Tables	5	$175
Paper Towel Dispenser	4	$50
Dishwasher	0	Already purchased ☺
Dish sprayer	1	$205
Dish rack	3	$25
Mandolin	1	$130
Mixer	1	$250
Convection Oven	0	Already purchased ☺
Heat Lamp	2	$140
Trash Cans	5	$80
Turners	4	$5

This is the spiel we would give during our meetings with potential board members.

"We love good healthy food and know not everyone has access to it. We want to open a café where you can pay whatever you can for a meal. Those with means could pay more to help someone else eat. Those without money could volunteer in the kitchen and learn some jobs skills along the way. It would be a dignified way of providing food access. It would build community. We have invested our life savings into the café. Can you join us in building community through healthy food access?"

A few people turned us down, but most people responded with a resounding, "YES!" At one point, someone asked us: "Why don't you just donate to an organization who is already doing something about food access like Food Bank of the Rockies?" Questions like that were our chance to let people know SAME Café would be different. We believed in this concept of building community around healthy and affordable food so much that we were willing to bet our life savings on it.

At that time, there were a few local organizations trying to tackle the issue of food access. There were food banks, soup kitchens, and daily church meals being offered. Not one of these places focused on healthy food or even what would actually help people in the long run. Most of them were set up to provide a free, emergency service. If you walked into a food bank, you would have been given a box of food that may or may not have met your dietary restrictions or preferences. You might walk into a soup kitchen on a day when they were serving spaghetti and meatballs and not be able to eat because you are gluten free and vegetarian. Just because someone is experiencing poverty does not mean they deserve less or they should just be thankful for what they get.

Yes, it is amazing there are agencies that can bridge a gap for people who are struggling. But imagine yourself in that situation. How good does it feel to be told what to eat or when to eat it? Most of us have choices every day that are taken for granted. When someone experiences poverty, immediately those choices are no longer available. Not only was there a lack of choice in these soup kitchens and food banks, but people often had to fill out a form to prove they needed the service. Then they would need to stand in a long line or make an appointment ahead of time to be served. None of these methods felt dignified to us. The idea was to approach each person who walked through the door as a dignified human being whether they had money for lunch or not.

We felt there was something magical about feeding people and sharing meals. The way we connect over food helps us create a sense of belonging. Eating with others can even reduce symptoms of depression. If you think back to your earliest memories of food, you probably weren't alone. That memory sticks because you were sharing that meal with others. Spending time cooking and preparing food and then sharing it with someone creates real intimacy. We open ourselves up to vulnerability by sharing food.

Having people over for dinner was one of our favorite things. It was so much fun thinking up a menu that would be pleasing to our guests. "What are their favorite foods? Do they eat meat? I don't think she eats onions. He isn't eating sugar right now." The entire evening would be focused on making our guests happy. Hopefully, at the end of the night, our guests would feel full. Not just satiated with food, but also with the conversation and the care that went into preparing the food. These were precious relationships.

Our goal with SAME Café was to treat every guest the same we would anyone we invited over for dinner. Dignity would be the secret. It would be the relationships we would build. This would be the thing that mattered and made SAME different from any other charity working on food access.

One of Libby's co-workers had lots of questions about how this was all going to play out. His wife was instantly excited about how SAME would be different from other charitable models. She had marketing skills we lacked and helped us create our first brochures and flyers. We asked her to serve as another founding member of our board. It wasn't until years later that she shared her husband thought this was a terrible idea and would never work. Thank God they didn't share that with us early on!

Shortly into this journey, we did lots of research and read a ton of books. From these readings, we took away questions like: How will we measure our days on this planet? Will it be in the amount of money saved over a lifetime? The number of cars we were able to buy? If we had a vacation house in the mountains? Or would it be the relationships we built and the chances we took? The most important thing we took from this introspection was you can't take money with you when you die.

We had had similar conversations with our family and friends when we talked to each one of them about SAME. What will matter most in the end is not what we have but what we gave and shared. We moved forward, even though apparently others were thinking this was a crazy idea. We knew it was crazy, but we weren't afraid to open SAME Café. We were afraid of how we would feel if we didn't.

We became obsessed with looking online through sites like Craigslist and Ebay. We scoured the listings for used equipment and spaces to rent. At thrift stores we found small items like plates and silverware. Through an online auction, we purchased a commercial coffee maker and a convection oven without a plug. A lot of time was spent driving around picking up all the pieces we still needed. A couple in a nearby suburb had just closed their restaurant, so we bought the triple sink from them that is still in use today. A coffee shop downtown was closing and sold us everything—and I mean everything —that was in their space. We got trash cans, Cambros (which are basically containers for holding food), spatulas, sheet pans, floor mats, paper goods and even a toilet. When we arrived in a borrowed box truck to pick up all the purchases, Libby asked me, "What the hell are we going to do with a used toilet?" This is how naïve we were—we had no idea what we might need, so we just took it all.

Our families spent hours scrubbing, organizing and finding places to store all of our purchases. Libby's sister Katie and her husband, Rich, had recently moved from Texas to Colorado and didn't live too far away from us. They offered their garage as our second storage space. The laundry room in our house was no longer for laundry but a storage center for supplies. At one point, Libby gave me the ultimatum that we had to find a location or get rid of the treasures because she couldn't get to the washer and dryer without holding laundry above her head. That became our impetus for biting the bullet and finding a space.

I remember being so nervous during our first real sit-down meeting to talk about SAME Café and drum up some support. Liesje was a parent of kids who attended Libby's school. She had a background in hospitality management and could bring some restaurant related expertise to the table. This woman was and still is an amazing cheerleader for us in every sense of the word. Liesje was one of the first people we thought to approach when we were looking for help in getting the café off the ground. We knew the kind of person she is and what she cares about in the world. She is one of those people who would do anything for anyone. She is kind, considerate, generous, down to earth, thoughtful, honest and helpful.

The meeting turned into a long-standing relationship with one of SAME Café's greatest supporters. We sat in her living room and poured out our idea. We told her why we felt so passionate about starting this café and just how we were going to do it (or so we thought). Even though she had true culinary credentials, she didn't laugh at us or question our motives. Instead, she wrote a check and signed on as one of our founding board members. At that point, I remember driving away from her beautiful home and Libby turning to me and saying, "Shit! This is really going to happen!"

Chapter 4

Open for Business

We found a commercial real estate agent and started looking at every empty space inside a grid we created on a Denver map. The location needed to be close to downtown, on a major bus line and in an area with an identified need but also with access to a population of people who could help. It needed to be diverse and accessible. Our first couple of locations were exciting to scope out; however, we quickly learned it couldn't be too big or too expensive.

At first, we thought we wanted a space already built out as a commercial kitchen, but again we learned that convenience comes with a price tag. When our families were in town, we would take them to potential spaces and get their opinions. There were three locations we were super excited about and almost signed leases on, but every time we got to the details of our business plan, landlords would run. Most of their responses were, "No soup kitchens in my space." Although we'd explain this model was nothing like a soup kitchen, all they could picture were lines of stereotypical homeless around the block.

On Craigslist, we saw an ad posted for a recently closed coffee shop right in the neighborhood where we wanted to be. The building manager met us there and showed us the space. It was filthy, and it was clear why the health department had recently shut them down. They were serving food without a food license and doing dishes in a tiny, bathroom-style sink. There was definitely some work that needed to be done, but it was in the right neighborhood and we could see potential in the space. It was dark and full of the equipment they had abandoned, nothing useful of course. We liked the size (600 square feet with a basement the same size) and decided to take a chance. We explained our business plan to the building manager, and he actually seemed excited. Little did we know, he was a formerly homeless individual who knew the neighborhood could use a place like SAME. He went to bat for us with the landlord and got us a face-to-face meeting with him. We were invited to his high-rise condo to discuss the plans.

We explained the concept, and waited with bated breath to hear his response. He was apprehensive, so we assured him we could pay a year's worth of rent up front. That seemed to impress him enough to agree. We signed a one-year lease and he handed us the keys. The first thing we did was walk straight over from that meeting to the new space to start cleaning it up. It desperately needed to be painted. The upstairs was dark brown on all the walls and ceiling. The basement floor was Christmas red and green. Our entire group of friends and family who were around pitched in and started painting and clearing stuff out.

Some of the spaces we had toured with the real estate agent had quite a bit of existing equipment still installed. That meant there would be no limit to the kinds of food we would have been able to prepare. However, the abandoned space was so sparse we were going to have to supply and install every piece of equipment ourselves. Due to our limited budget for purchasing equipment, we decided to keep the offerings simple and approachable—pizza, soup, and salad. Diners could finish their meal with one of our favorite dessert items—a shortbread cookie.

Can we talk about the cookies for a minute? These cookies were one of Libby's family recipes and we knew from the start we would be serving them in the café. You would think a simple shortbread cookie couldn't be that tasty, but these are simply amazing. Originally, the cookies were topped with a butter and shortening icing —not exactly a beacon of healthiness. Our version replaced that with a simple combination of lemon juice and powdered sugar. The combination of sweet and sour match perfectly with the rich, buttery shortbread and are the perfect way to end a meal.

The menu was not just devised around kitchen equipment. Pizza seemed to be an approachable item that could be varied in lots of ways. It was a great vehicle for delivering a wide array of ingredients, including some less popular vegetables. We imagined most people would be willing to try a slice of pizza even if we were putting healthy ingredients like kale or eggplant on it. As with pizza, the soups and salads could also be endlessly varied. It was important that the limited menu still changed enough each day that customers wouldn't get bored.

The simple menu meant we would only need an oven to bake the pizzas and cookies and a couple of soup warmers. One really good thing we discovered was since we would be using an electric oven, according to the building code at the time, we wouldn't need a ventilation hood over the oven. This was great news for us since installing something like that would have been a huge expense.

This was the summer of 2006. Libby was off from teaching, and we were spending almost every spare moment inside the café space. Along with Katie and Rich, my younger sister, Angie, lived in the area and would regularly come by to help us paint and set things up. We were excited that we would be opening soon, or so we thought.

Little did we know opening a unique restaurant isn't that easy. In between painting and cleaning out the space, we were desperately trying to figure out how to open a non-profit restaurant. We would go down to City Hall almost every day to ask questions about permits and inspections and were often passed from one department to another. No one knew exactly what to do with a non-profit café. Each time we'd get a "No" from one city employee, we'd just go back another day and ask someone else. Usually, we could find a sympathetic ear who was willing to help us limp along in the process.

Even though we were not changing anything structurally, we were required to obtain architectural drawings, which meant we needed an architect. One of our friends knew someone who was willing to help us out. He designed the interior layout of the kitchen and customer space. He also used his architect magic to get it all entered into software to create a printout we could have on file with the building department.

We were three months in by the time this hurdle was jumped, and Libby was already heading back to school. Luckily, Denise Cerreta from One World Café in Salt Lake City came to town as promised that fall. She rented a room around the corner from the café space. She was an incredible addition and helped us with laying tile, making curtains and painting. She was also able to hang out and wait for deliveries and inspections while Libby and I were at work. One day Denise took some flyers around to the businesses and homes in the area announcing the café. She explained the concept, so they knew what to expect from their new neighbors.

One of the last issues we had to overcome was due to a lingering line in the Denver code. The line specified how much fresh air was required to be present in a public space in order to prevent Legionnaire's Disease.

We had never even heard of this disease and wondered how it was still a line item in Denver Code. Is that really something we needed to be worried about in 2006? We were told we needed to have an air handling unit installed that would pump in a certain amount of outside air each minute. Since the outside temperatures in Denver vary greatly, the unit would have to have the ability to heat and cool the incoming air. Of course, that meant it was going to cost thousands. The problem was, since the renovations had been taking months longer than we originally planned, we didn't have that kind of money left. We were down to our last dollars, and the idea that we were going to be stopped in our tracks when we were finally getting so close just about crushed us. Libby broke down in tears talking to our architect, and we really thought we might never get to open and make one meal. Eventually, one sympathetic official was able to approve our existing windows and doors as sources of fresh air. We finally had our approvals and were able to open for business!

The final product was a bright and airy place. Thanks to family and friends, the walls were painted a buttery yellow. The new color coordinated well with the original brown color of the ceiling. We weren't brave enough to tackle painting the ceiling since the walls were over fourteen feet high. We had the triple sink we bought on Craigslist installed on a long wall. The electric pizza oven was on the lower shelf of a stainless-steel table and two soup pots were on top. We had seventeen seats with five tall tables that looked into the kitchen space and three small tables up front. There was a refrigerated deli case left in the space we used as a boundary to the kitchen and also to hold salads. A vegetable prep sink was on the back wall and the rest of the kitchen was just stainless-steel tables and storage.

The first time we showed Katie the space, we were determined to clear out some of the old useless furnishings. There was a huge banquette in the middle of the space that needed to be moved to the dumpster. After carefully measuring, we figured out it would just barely fit through the back door but only if we took the door off its hinges. We began the work of maneuvering it out, Katie at one end, and Libby and I at the other. We got it to the doorway and it was so tight that every inch was scraping on the door as we pushed as hard as we could.

The piece was somewhat wedged in the doorway and we were exhausted. We were taking a break when a woman stuck her head in the back door and asked if we needed some help. We didn't want anyone we didn't know getting injured in the café, so we told the woman we could manage. But she just wouldn't let it go. She kept insisting that she was really strong. Libby and I finally gave in, and this stranger was actually a great help.

It was hard work, and we were all sweating by the time that banquette was out the back door. She asked for some water. We didn't have cups or anything else in the space yet, but I had a water bottle and so did Libby. We filled one of our water bottles from the bathroom sink and gave it to her. It was a hot Denver day, and I told her she could take the water bottle with her if she wanted. She was totally floored that we would give her one of our bottles.

She sat down on the curb and introduced herself as Patti. Her teeth were rotting and her rusty red hair hadn't seen a brush in a while, but that didn't deter her from making friends with us that day. She told us she was a fifty something year old heroin addict who has had several bouts with homelessness. She was a regular at a day shelter for women and children just down the road. She came through the neighborhood for her methadone treatments and had clearly seen better days. We explained the concept of the café and she fell in love immediately. She promised she would be one of our first customers and kept that promise.

Patti was such a perfect person for SAME Café. She cared about helping and having a place to belong. She was one of those people we hoped to help from the beginning. She wanted to work for her food. She didn't want a hand-out. Of course, she had her good days and her bad days, but she loved that she belonged at SAME. She loved that people knew her name. She was part of something. She hugged us every time we saw her. More than a decade later, Patti still comes around SAME. Her greeting that day and every time she came in was, "Hey, hey, hey," just like Dwayne from *What's Happening*. Katie and Libby still greet each other that way sometimes and grin, remembering that day in the alley when they first met our friend Patti.

Katie and Rich were invaluable in those early days. In addition to storing a bunch of our equipment and helping us renovate the space, Katie and Libby spent hours creating art for the walls. They painted 1x8 inch boards to match the wall colors and mounted quotes that each board member selected. Rich volunteered to help set up the accounting software and diligently helped us with the bookkeeping for years.

They even helped us plan a soft opening with a bunch of their friends. We invited people to come try SAME Café and give us feedback on what they experienced. It would be our first time serving anyone in the newly renovated space. Even though it certainly didn't scream professional restaurant kitchen, we were determined to make it work.

As guests of Katie and Rich began to arrive, our nerves and excitement were peaking. We were really doing this! All of us were busily greeting and serving customers. People were making selections from our menu of two soups, two salads and two kinds of pizza. We were plating food as fast as we could. Thankfully, Katie and Rich jumped in to help. Things were so hectic that no one noticed at one point Libby was on the floor behind the counter. She had reached down to a floor outlet to plug in a hot plate and was zapped with electricity. She bounced back up and acted as if nothing happened. When everything was said and done, we had served over sixty customers, and Libby said her hand was still a little tingly.

The feedback we got that day was priceless. Customers were honest and fair even though they were friends of Katie and Rich. We realized how important it was to have a clear message about the pay-what-you-can system. To help with that, Libby created a sign that sat on the front counter explaining how the café worked. We also got good suggestions on portion size and number of menu selections. And of course, everyone loved the cookies!

After spending some time processing this feedback and changing a few things, on October 20, 2006, we officially opened. There was no fanfare around the opening because we really didn't announce it to anyone. When 11am rolled around we simply flipped the open sign and waited to see who showed up. It was a Friday, and Libby had taken the day off from teaching so we could experience it together. I think we served about nine people that first official day. It was interesting watching people's faces as we did our best to explain this new concept. Most of them worked in the nearby neighborhood businesses who were more curious than anything about the new kids on the block.

Each day after that, Libby would call at the end of her school day to hear how things went. I would give her the rundown of who came into the café and what I made for lunch. At the time, we were only serving about ten people a day. It was easy enough to stop at the grocery store to get supplies on our way to the café in the morning. Libby would drop me off and head to school. I would get busy making pizza dough, chopping veggies and making soup.

At the end of the school day when Libby was finished grading papers and planning, she would come to the café, clean-up whatever mess I left or make cookie dough for the next day and count the money in the box. Often, she would answer emails and snail mail until nine or ten o'clock at night. While she was cleaning up my mess, I would be downtown working my "real" job. The contract job I had was willing to let me come in after the café closed. Both of us keeping our jobs gave us a bit of stability with a regular paycheck and health insurance since we weren't getting paid to work at the café.

I remember one time she called me from SAME while I was working my office job. She was so excited when I answered the phone, at first, I thought something was wrong. She just kept yelling in this high-pitched voice, "You'll never believe this!" When she was finally able to calm down, she told me when she opened the box to count it, she found a hundred dollar bill. I was shocked. We talked about the day and rehashed almost every interaction I had with customers. I had no idea which customer could have left that in the box. It was so inspiring and mind-blowing to know that someone had donated so much. This happened quite a few times throughout our years and every time it was awesome. It reinforced our belief that this idea would work.

Within the first few weeks of opening, Libby's Aunt Kate and Uncle Phil came from San Diego to help get things in order. They had run a bed and breakfast for decades and had great tips for us.

Every day, Uncle Phil would find a project and walk down to the thrift store just a block away and pick up any necessary parts or pieces he needed. They hung a huge mirror right inside the door to make the space look bigger—that mirror hung in that spot for over ten years. Aunt Kate bought seasonal decorations to spruce the place up and had tons of tips on record keeping and how to stay on top of things.

When Uncle Phil wasn't fixing something or organizing our tool closet, he was folding origami paper cranes. He folded large paper cranes and small ones and even tiny ones. There were cranes flying gracefully over the service area, kitchen, dish pit and even the basement. They tucked paper cranes on shelves in our office and in little cubbies in our storage area. Every time I'd come across one of those cranes, I'd think of how much they supported and helped us. I think of Uncle Phil and Aunt Kate every time I see a paper crane. Libby still carries some of the original paper cranes in her wallet.

Aunt Kate loved to tell the story of the time she and Uncle Phil flew from California to Illinois to attend a wedding. They had no idea there was an article about SAME Café in the airline magazine. They had been on the flight for three hours and were just about to land. The flight attendant told them to put their seatbacks up and tray tables away as Uncle Phil flipped to the story of SAME Café.

Aunt Kate saw the article and as Libby tells it, "She wigged out!" We hadn't mentioned it to anyone because we weren't sure if it was even going to get published. As they were exiting the plane, Aunt Kate bragged to everyone around her that the article was about her niece and nephew. She collected as many copies of the magazine as she could on her way off the plane. She sent us multiple copies, sent some to Libby's sisters, and even sent all her own siblings a copy.

Chapter 5

Miracles

In those first few days we were open, there were so many times when we would come across a roadblock and be amazed at how the universe was able to solve so many problems for us. I can remember in the very first week, someone called and wanted to order ten entire pizzas to go the following Thursday. They asked if we were up to the challenge, and we accepted.

Up to this point, when someone wanted a whole pizza, we would send it out on a dinner plate wrapped in aluminum foil. I know what you're thinking, "You didn't buy pizza boxes?" We hadn't thought of that just yet. We really thought people would just order pizza by the slice and stay in to eat it. We had not even imagined people would want to take pizza out and certainly not entire pizzas to go.

Immediately, we got online and ordered pizza boxes. The order confirmation said the boxes would arrive that following Friday, the day after the big to go order. We were bummed but knew there would be other orders when those boxes would come in handy. Thursday arrived, and we started fulfilling the ten pizza to go order. We were putting them on dinner plates and started to wrap them in aluminum foil as the UPS driver came through the front door with our order of boxes. They arrived a day early and just in time for the pick-up.

Around March of 2007, a group of women came in to have cookies and coffee. They had just been to a local restaurant for lunch to celebrate one of their ninety-first birthdays and were reading about SAME in the local paper. They asked to speak to one of the Birkys, and I introduced myself. One of the women in the group, Hazel, wanted to know if I knew any Birkys from Central Illinois. Hazel had taught at a one room schoolhouse in Antioch, Illinois with a Simon Birky. She wondered if I knew him. She would have worked at the school right around 1940. Flabbergasted, I told her that Simon Birky was my grandfather, and I knew he had been superintendent of that school. This was a crazy coincidence. (Though Libby always says there are no such things as coincidences.) She asked if my grandparents were still living, and I told her my grandfather had died in 1993 but Grandma Birky was still alive. She asked if I could connect them, so I took down her address. The two became penpals writing many letters back and forth over the years, filling each other in on their lives. The string of coincidence does not end there.

In 2009, we moved into a new house and called Grandma Birky to give her our new address. She was taken aback and said she thought Hazel might be our neighbor. Knowing my Grandma was ninety-two, I didn't think much of what she said, but she got out her address book and told me Hazel's exact address. It turns out we bought a house four doors down from Hazel in a city of more than a million people. The chances of that! We marched ourselves right down to Hazel's house and re-introduced ourselves. From that moment on, we became special friends and occasionally caregivers to this beautifully smart human being. She earned her PhD In education back when women were barely allowed to work outside the home. Hazel had outlived almost all her familial connections, of which she had few since she was adopted as a child and never got married. So quickly we became like family.

At the time of writing this, Hazel recently passed away in her home just shy of 104 years old. We were still very involved in her life all the way until the end. We made sure she got to spend her last days on Earth in her home, which was what she wanted. No matter how one might explain the series of events that connected us, Hazel was a moving presence in our lives since the day she walked into SAME Café.

Another amazing miracle happened when a young woman called and asked if we would be willing to host her baby shower. Luckily Libby was there so I could give her the phone, as this was far from my area of expertise. The caller had read about SAME Café in one of the recent articles. She was adamant about having it at SAME because of the mission and philosophy. She thought it would be a cool connection to have her baby shower be more than just people giving her presents. Libby explained to her that we only had seventeen seats, and she wanted to invite forty women to this event. The space was very limited, and it didn't seem to make sense. The caller asked Libby if we had any space anywhere else like in a basement.

Early on, our basement was just an unfinished space. It was not baby shower material. We were using the basement as overflow to store extra equipment, those pizza boxes and some pantry items. It did have some tables and chairs, but they were the discards from upstairs. They were all broken or wobbly and ugly and stained. We didn't even own forty chairs total in the entire space.

Libby described the space to the woman, explaining it was no place to have a baby shower. Even I would not recommend having a baby shower there. The caller shared with Libby that she lived in the mountains and would be unable to come see it before the party. She wasn't worried. Libby assured her it wouldn't be perfect and she SHOULD be worried. First, it was full of all the crap left from the previous tenant along with our collection. Second, those steps leading to the basement were downright dangerous. Again, she wasn't worried. Libby begrudgingly agreed and said we'd see her soon.

Libby's sister Katie agreed to come and help us clean out the space. Libby went to the nearest big box store and bought forty matching folding chairs. We hung some Christmas lights and tried to clear out the space as best we could.

The first winter SAME Café was open was particularly snowy, even for Denver. There were several big snowstorms that unloaded snow and ice upon the city. After each snowfall, legions of entrepreneurs would comb the city streets trying to earn a few bucks by clearing sidewalks and driveways for both homeowners and businesses alike. It was on one of those days that we first met Kidd. He had just finished shoveling for one of the few folks who already knew about SAME, and she suggested that he might like to come over to the café for a hot meal.

I'll never forget what he looked like when Kidd first walked through the door. He was bulked up with at least three coats, ragged and torn boots on his feet, ice crystals in his scraggly beard, and a worn trucker style hat on top of a mop of rusty, long, brown hair. We had already shoveled the sidewalk outside the front door that day, so he put a couple of dollars in the donation box and ordered his lunch. He didn't talk much at first, but before he left, he introduced himself and asked if he could come by again the next time it snowed and shovel our sidewalk in exchange for a meal.

Several snowstorms happened in the next few weeks, and each time we would arrive at SAME in the morning to find the sidewalk already shoveled AND a path cleared from our back door to our parking space. On those days Kidd would come back after we opened and order his lunch—usually a plate heavy on the greens and vegetables, a large mug of soup and maybe a slice of pizza. He loved the fresh greens more than anything; he explained he rarely had the chance to eat something that didn't come out of a can. We found out he was sleeping in the park a few blocks away rather than a shelter, covering himself with a tarp and feeding the ducks with food people gave him. In his experience, the shelters were full of things he didn't love—thieves, bugs and addicts—and he didn't want to be around those elements. He would rather huddle under a tree or bush in the park inside his sleeping bag and brave the cold.

Time and time again Kidd would come, and we would talk during the slow afternoon hours. He told me he was shoveling and doing odd jobs around town so he could save up enough money to get back to his hometown of New Orleans, where he wanted to help with Hurricane Katrina clean up. He had previously been a live-in custodial worker at one of the local churches there, but had been displaced by the hurricane when it came through and destroyed his workplace/home. He was evacuated to Denver in order to escape the worst of the destruction, but now that the Gulf area was beginning to be safe enough for folks to return, he was anxious to get back.

On the day he came in to show me the ticket and say goodbye, I almost didn't recognize him. The clean-cut man wearing freshly laundered jeans, a button-down shirt and new work boots looked nothing like the Kidd we had come to know. The bushy beard was gone, only a well-trimmed mustache remained. It was only the trucker hat and the sparkle in his eyes that gave him away. He was on his way out of town but couldn't leave without stopping in first to say goodbye. When he found out Libby wasn't at the café that day, he promised to come back on Saturday before heading out of town.

When Libby finally saw him, she couldn't believe her eyes. Could this possibly be the same guy? She was amazed at his transformation, but even more than that, she was amazed at his gratitude for SAME. After Kidd ate, we hugged him and made sure to give him our address so he could write, even though we wondered if he ever would.

The day of the party came, and we weren't sure how we were going to improve the space anymore. It happened to be a day when we were not regularly open which was good because we were not just hosting the party in our space but making all the food. We arrived early in the morning knowing the group would arrive around 1:00 for a 2:00 shower.

At that point, Libby was pretty much panicking. There was a big shelf full of extra things that really needed to be covered up somehow. Katie had a great idea to walk down the street to the local thrift store and buy a bunch of sheets to cover up the shelf. At the store they found a tablecloth, a shower curtain, a piece of random fabric and a bed sheet all in similar shades of green. They were all folded up and stapled so they had no idea if they were the right size. The pieces didn't exactly match but they were close enough. Libby thought, "OK, these will have to do." The two of them ended up buying every piece of fabric they could find in the same shade of green. Katie and Libby brainstormed ways they could make the pieces work—folding them up if they were too long or tucking them in. They looked for curtain rods but didn't really find any. I was sure there was something in the basement that could work.

Katie and Libby knew time was running out, so they went to work. Magically the material they bought fit perfectly around the shelves and hung on curtain rods I found in the piles of stuff left behind. Every piece of fabric was the exact right length and width for what they needed. They finished covering up the shelves just as the ladies were coming down the steps to set up. The baby shower turned out to be beautiful, and no one died going down those steps as I had feared. The mommy-to-be was so excited to have been able to have her baby shower take place in a non-profit.

Although we weren't officially a non-profit yet, we had turned in our IRS paperwork back in April of 2006. The paperwork came back to us a couple of times requesting more information. We went back and forth a few times but knew we could open without it. If we were granted non-profit status, it would be retroactive. We kept explaining our idea to the IRS, but since this was a unique idea and new to everyone, they weren't exactly sure what to do with us. Enter Patrick.

Patrick was one of our first regular volunteers. He was grateful for the delicious meals and volunteered in exchange most days. I would talk to him about how he was going to be working in the mountains as a ski instructor. Each day, he would wander in with his day pack and cozy up to a table. His long scruffy beard disguised his sweet smile.

Patrick and I worked together most days while he was in town. As we got to know each other better, he mentioned he was a retired tax attorney and willing to go over the non-profit paperwork with us. He was amazing! He spent hours at the library reading up and walking us through our application. He delivered lots of highlighted pages and notes from his time at the library. Shortly after that, he disappeared into the mountains, and thanks to his help, our application was finally approved.

Every so often when we would come into the café and turn on the lights and start to get things prepared for the day, we would find small bills on the floor near the front door. A couple of times a month, we'd find dollar bills strewn about in front of the entrance just inside the door. At first, we thought we were dropping money out of the donation box on the way to the basement to count it. Only after the second or third time did we realize someone was pushing money through the mail slot after we had closed.

We often wondered who this person was. One night we were closing after a late evening with a church group who rented the space for a meeting. We heard a noise by the front door and saw a gentleman in the process of inserting money. When he realized we were there, he tried to move on quickly, but we opened the door and invited him in. The man shared that he could never make it over when we were open because he was working day labor. He said he didn't have much, but whenever he was blessed, he felt compelled to share it. We thanked the donor and he quickly went on his way. After he was gone, Libby and I just looked at each other, totally overwhelmed with gratitude for this generous human. That was not the last time we saw him or found a few dollars on the floor before opening.

At the time, we were driving our own vehicle for all the café needs. Daily, we were hauling compost to the local community garden, going to the grocery store, and picking up vegetables from the few local farms who were helping. We put on the wish list that SAME could use a vehicle. A local food pantry had just been gifted a new refrigerated truck and would no longer be needing an older, multicolored minivan with tinted windows and asked us if it could work for SAME. The vehicle needed a lot of things, including new brakes and tires. It had a cracked windshield, and the license plate was duct taped in the back window. There were no back seats so the van was perfect for hauling compost and veggies—or children. We nick named it the "kidnapper van" after we were pulled over in the vehicle three times in three months.

We were thrilled to have the new addition to SAME Café. When anyone came in, we'd share with them about the new ride. We wrote about the gift in the newsletter. One of the regular customers came in and asked to see the van. Of course, we marched him right out the back door to proudly show it off. He was immediately unimpressed and so worried for our safety he offered to buy the café a brand-new vehicle. His family had a foundation that was looking to collaborate with a smaller organization where they could see their dollars make a difference. We were able to go to the dealership and pick out exactly what SAME needed. The minivan was then "gifted" to another non-profit. We ended up driving home a new, small pick-up truck that could drive in snow and haul anything the café needed.

Chapter 6

In the News

The local neighborhood paper ran a story on SAME right away which helped spread the word. This was great because we chose not to advertise in those first few months. Because Libby was still teaching, I was doing most of the weekday work myself. It was a good thing that the café wasn't that busy. The slower pace of those first months gave us the time to refine our daily routines so we would be ready when the crowds started to roll in, hopefully. The slow natural growth took place over the first few months, but then more articles started going to print.

One of the first articles was in the *Westword*, which is a local entertainment style magazine. The food critic called when I was on the bus heading uptown from my "real" job to the café. On this day, I headed into the office before going to SAME. It was a crazy snowy day and I was anticipating a slow day at the café. Weather always affected our numbers. I talked to him and explained the concept and he seemed skeptical. The article that was finally printed shared his skepticism—his

—

last sentence stated he doubted that SAME Café would last very long.

At first, we were insulted, hurt by that comment and angry. What did he know? He had never even stepped foot inside the café as far as we knew. It certainly fueled our fire to prove him and all the skeptics wrong. We already knew he was wrong. Even in our first few months of being open, there were so many stories to show the effort it took to open was worth it.

Aussie John described his life as a roller coaster—with some wonderful highs and some demoralizing lows. He was born in Texas but spent many of his adult years in Australia. His voice had that distinct Aussie accent although he had been back in the States for over a decade. He openly talked about his struggles with alcohol and living with HIV. He first heard about SAME Café through a day shelter for people who are experiencing homelessness and are HIV+.

He said he fell in love with SAME on day one. John loved the opportunity to access high end, mostly organic fare and to be part of a grass roots movement. The food is the number one reason he kept coming back, but he also enjoyed the feeling of being part of something greater than himself.

John had no regular income, so instead, he helped through the physical contribution of volunteering. He was an enthusiastic and thorough dishwasher. There was a level of accountability to the volunteer sign up process he appreciated. He knew if he put his name down for a shift, then there was an expectation and a need for him to be at the café on time and ready to work.

John was the type of customer that felt so integrated into the community, he would say "we", "us" and "ours" when he talked about SAME Café. He knew he mattered there. It might have been one of the only places in the world where that was still the case for him. Each day when he walked through the door, he was greeted by name and acknowledged for the person he was and the contributions he made. Each day he was seen. He was not invisible. He was needed.

We wish the author of that *Westword* article had taken the time to see the intention was more than a café. It probably seemed absurd to him, or anyone with restaurant experience, that a café with no set prices would be successful. His article missed the magic of what it was to be part of a café like SAME.

SAME Café is, and will always be, more than a typical restaurant. It is a place where Kidd, Patti and John are welcome and encouraged to thrive. As much as Kidd, Patti, and John needed SAME, SAME needed them. The fact that so many different folks found SAME Café a place to belong and be fulfilled just proved it was needed. Community was integral to making the café work day after day. It still is.

We were sure there were more naysayers out there. This *Westword* writer happened to put his doubts into print. We thought at first his article might hurt us, but as Libby's sister always said, "All press is good press." It turns out his article just led to more articles. It's funny how perspectives can change. One year later, the same journalist wrote another article that reviewed our first successful year. During his second article about the café, he "gladly ate his words." His second article reflected on how wrong he had been.

Another journalist heard there were now two cafés (Denver and Salt Lake City) with flexible payment systems. She authored an article for *TIME Magazine's* online site that went to print the day after Christmas, just two months after SAME had opened. The irony of the timing was we had decided to close the café over the holidays so we could head home to be with our families. Being naïve, we had used my cell phone as the main café phone number. Even though we were 1,000 miles away from SAME, we started to get phone calls from people who had seen the article and wanted more information.

One of those calls was from a radio station in Quebec (yes, the Canadian one) that wanted to do a live phone interview. We were totally caught off guard. Neither of us had expected that kind of response and we were not experienced in public speaking. However, we also weren't about to turn down such an amazing opportunity to spread the word, so we agreed to do the interview. It probably helped that we knew if we choked, the audience was an entire country away. The interview went relatively well and was good practice for the future.

Another of the calls during that holiday break was from someone who had read the article and subsequently visited the website but couldn't find anywhere they could donate online. When the site was built, we were still waiting to hear if the IRS 501(c)(3) designation was going to be approved, so we hadn't yet set up such a system. Now that we knew there were people who wanted to donate, I didn't waste any time getting a button added to the website to make it possible.

Once we returned from our holiday with our families, the days were busier. More customers were calling, coming in and emailing. There was more news coverage with an article in the *Denver Post* and we were featured on Colorado Public Radio. I was trying to keep up with the demand during the weekday while Libby was at school. Naturally, customers would pitch in to help when they saw me in there by myself. Slowly, folks started to offer to come in to help open or make food and the volunteer program began to develop.

Gradually, with Libby's help, I started to formalize the volunteer process. I would ask folks ahead of time if they would plan to volunteer the next day and put together a binder that contained the schedule. Instead of just depending on the luck of the draw, I was able to count on people on specific days.

I was still working my consulting gig. Each day, when I came in, most of the other consultants were heading home for the day. My co-workers, Richard and Darin, were interested in the café and would regularly ask how things were going. Darin had spent a lot of years working in a large chain restaurant, so he knew the restaurant life well. He was also a talented cook. The two of us would often bring in samples of our latest concoctions for the other to taste. More than once, Darin came in and put his skills to use by helping out in the café kitchen.

Richard was an avid skydiver and risk taker, so he was intrigued by the risks we were taking. He wanted to see it up close and offered to come and help one Saturday. It was a busy day, so Richard got to see the café in full swing. We put him to work on various tasks but like most people he eventually ended up on the dish station. Despite the numerous warnings and signage, Richard had a momentary lapse in judgement and emptied all three of the sink basins at one time. Due to the age of the building and the limitations of our renovation budget, this was a recipe for disaster. The small drain lines and floor sink couldn't hold all the water. Instantly we were walking in a two-inch puddle that went all the way out the front door and caused it to rain into the basement. He wasn't the first, nor was he the last, to flood the kitchen. We used to joke volunteers could earn a button ("I volunteered at SAME Café and I didn't flood the kitchen!") if they completed a shift without a mishap.

Bob loved beans. Whenever we had an item with beans on the menu, there was no doubt which item Bob would order. Black bean soup and three bean salad were two of his absolute favorites. He first started coming into SAME in early spring of 2007 when the snow still occasionally fell. Salty and slushy footprints were constantly appearing in the dining area, and as a retired janitor, Bob was no stranger to a broom and mop. He would often jump into action after he finished his lunch and help keep the floors tidied up and looking their best.

When Bob's wife retired, she started to join him on his daily trek across Colfax Avenue to dine at the café. They lived in an apartment complex for seniors two blocks away. Since they were on a fixed income, it was convenient for them to come and eat at SAME and leave a donation.

Bob shared with us he was a recovering alcoholic, over thirty years sober. He attended meetings regularly at the Alcoholics Anonymous club located just a few blocks from SAME Café. He taught us quite a lot about AA and what it is like to be a recovering addict. He only liked to celebrate his AA birthday rather than his "belly button birthday," because according to him, the sober years were the only ones that mattered.

Once Bob realized Libby was coming in after school hours to prep food and clean the café so I could go back to the office, he offered to be our volunteer janitor. He would come in after we closed, clean the floors and finish up any dishes, and then all Libby would have to do is prep pizza dough and cookies for the following day and answer any snail mail or email. It was a great arrangement because we needed the help and Bob needed lunch.

In April of 2007, two significant things happened for SAME Café. First, that was the month when the IRS 501(c)(3) status became official, which meant we could finally start applying for grants. Second, was an article about SAME published in the *LA Times*. Not only was it in the *LA Times*, but it was in the Sunday edition on the front page with the headline visible above the fold, which is just about the best placement you could ever receive from a newspaper article.

We learned press coverage often leads to more press coverage. From that *LA Times* article sprang several radio and blog interviews. The *Rocky Mountain News* printed an article that not only talked about the café, but also featured the stories of two regular volunteers I mentioned earlier—Patti and Bob. The article featured a picture of Patti standing on the toilet wearing yellow rubber gloves and scrubbing away at the bathroom walls. She was so proud of that picture, and she still talks about it to this day.

That press coverage even led to a live appearance on the *CBS Saturday Early Show*. By the way, they aren't joking when they say "Early"—we had to be at the café, dressed and ready to shoot by 4am! The spot itself probably took less than two minutes, but hours to prepare for. It was the first time either of us had been on live national television. It was such a blur that I have no idea what we actually said, but I think we managed to make it through without any major stumbles.

There was a great article printed in the *American Way* inflight magazine in June of 2007. This is the article that Aunt Kate and Uncle Phil read while they were traveling to the Midwest. The author had interviewed us months before. He set it up ahead of time that he would fly to Denver to come and volunteer. He wanted to get his hands dirty and work at the café and then write his article from the perspective of a café volunteer. He wanted to give the viewpoint from behind the counter. That was the first time anyone had done anything like that. We had talked to writers about the café, but nobody had actually come in, volunteered, eaten and experienced the whole thing.

Libby thought it was hilarious that he included a particular interaction in his article. Whenever anyone came into the kitchen, she would always give them the same spiel, "Do a really good job washing the dishes because I am super anal, and I will make you wash them twice if they aren't clean." She shared her regular spiel with this reporter just like any other volunteer. She told him, "I have really high standards. I will make you wash them twice." He quoted her in the article and shared that he, indeed, had to wash some dishes twice.

We loved that he was willing to truly experience what it was like at SAME Café before writing. I think he was the first reporter to capture the heart and essence of what the café was and the whole idea behind it. All the articles did a good job talking about it, but there were always little things that did not quite click. It seemed like they didn't quite get it. Even just the way someone expressed it in written form sometimes rubbed us the wrong way and we would think to ourselves, "Nope, they don't get it. They don't understand." He was the first reporter to understand SAME, and whose writing reflected the way Libby and I saw the café. His article captured the spirit of the café. Still to this day, it is one of our favorite articles.

That July there was an article in the *Denver Catholic Register* about SAME Café. The article was not only published in the Denver area, but it was also circulated in Catholic newspapers all over the country. One of the Los Angeles area couples that happened to read the article became great supporters of SAME. While they lived in LA most of the year, they came back to Denver as often as they could. They would come to see local relatives and enjoy the clean mountain air. Soon after reading the article, Mary and Shadan planned their next trip to Denver to include a visit to SAME Café.

They happened to arrive on a slower day, so we were able to converse quite a bit while they were volunteering. We found out Mary was a high school math teacher, and Shadan worked for an aerospace company. The day they chose to come and volunteer happened to be Shadan's birthday. We also found out we had a mutual love for board games and trivia, so we had a ton to talk about.

From then on, each time one or both would come to town, we could count on them coming into SAME for a lunchtime visit. They often brought gifts for SAME they saw on the online wish list or they knew we would find useful. One time Mary brought Libby a pack of Sharpie markers with every color of the rainbow. From the look on Libby's face, you would have thought someone handed her a winning lottery ticket! They still visit SAME when they are in town, all thanks to that *Catholic Register* article.

Chapter 7
Meet the Neighbors

When SAME Café first opened on Colfax Avenue, it was the type of street that had a reputation. You never knew what you were going to see. *Playboy* magazine called it the "longest and wickedest" street in America. One of our favorite characters was the man who road a two-story tall bike while wearing a stove pipe hat, dressed like Uncle Sam. Whenever he, or any other strange sight, was visible through the café's front window, the regulars would look at each other, shrug, and say, "That's Colfax for ya!"

Rose was a regular customer from the beginning. She used to walk by daily to another destination and loved watching construction being done to the store front that eventually housed SAME Café. She told me once she was so glad something new was going in on this block of Colfax. She was impressed to see what was inside when it finally opened. She says she felt comfortable right away because of the friendly, efficient service from the staff. She was intrigued by the concept and thought it was just what was needed in our diversified neighborhood. She and I often talked about rising unemployment and how food banks were being depleted quickly now that there were more hungry mouths than ever.

She wrote an article once for our newsletter I thought I would share in part because she wrote with such enthusiasm. I included her words here because it is powerful to hear Rose's reaction.

> "With the SAME Café, anyone who is hungry may enter. It lets someone keep their dignity in allowing them to work for their meal by doing volunteer work, or if you are able to pay, you pay what you think your meal is worth. There is no set price! With the food being all organic, which consists of two salads, two soups and two styles of pizza on a daily basis, you can't go wrong. Healthy, affordable and caring about others at the same time. It doesn't get much better than that.
>
> With that said and done, it's my reason to keep returning. I have also learned to eat healthier and am feeling much better

having lost a few extra pounds. My daughter and grandchildren have been in a few times with me. Along with eating a good meal and providing dignity back into people's lives, the SAME Café also has displayed works of art colleagues and myself (have created) which helps us financially. The old saying "starving artist" still applies these days. I try to contribute to this great cause by being a steady customer and doing volunteer work when time allows..."

The café was in the middle of a cluster of first floor retail businesses in a mixed-use building three stories tall. The first floor included a boutique clothing store, a copy/fax/business supply store, a tanning salon and a karate studio. The upper floors contained forty studio and one-bedroom apartments. The businesses on the first floor were all struggling in a changing neighborhood. One by one, the businesses on our block began to close. Some of them relocated to the suburbs so the owners were closer to home, and other stores just didn't have enough customers to pay the rent.

The copy/fax shop right next door to SAME closed in the middle of 2007, and not too long afterwards, the tanning salon followed suit. We were quite nervous as to who our new neighbors might be. At one point, it seemed like our worries might be validated when a hand painted wooden sign proclaiming "Cigarette Store Coming Soon" appeared in the window of the space next door. That turned out to be a last-ditch effort from the renter to sublet his space, but the landlord got wind of it and intervened.

Being located on the main street of a major metropolitan city meant there were sometimes challenges. More than once, we came in to find our back door step had been used as a restroom. Our landlord required us to have extra glass insurance since broken windows was such a common occurrence. Stores in that area were constantly being tagged by graffiti artists and dumpsters were often ransacked or overflowing with abandoned mattresses.

One of our favorite neighbors, Herbs and Arts, came to our rescue one day after someone decided to take advantage of our donation box system and help themselves to the entire box. We were shocked to find the nice gentleman who asked for a glass of water would take the box and run into a waiting SUV in the alley. We were also shocked when every person in the café dropped what they were doing and took off after him. Plates of food were abandoned and dirty dishes left in the sink as, without a word, everyone realized what had happened and took off together.

After a failed attempt to chase him down, we returned to the café and called 911. They tried in vain to find the suspects, but never found them. The loss of the donation box itself was more upsetting than whatever money may have been in it. Libby's mom had handmade that box and gifted it to us for our opening day. We were both a little shaken up by the incident and closed for the rest of the day. We put a sign on the door indicating as such and went home. Upon returning the next day, our friends at Herbs and Arts came down and gave us the greatest hugs. They brought with them a huge, heavy cauldron to replace our donation box and sage to perform a cleansing ritual on the space. We felt so loved and supported!

Very early on we were visited by a Colfax regular named Daniel. Daniel was the first person we encountered who struggled with mental health and substance abuse issues. During our encounters with him, he was often inappropriate, aggressive and dangerous. He was notorious in the neighborhood. The woman that owned and ran the boutique next door often tried to pacify him by giving him a few dollars now and then or buying him burritos and bowls of green chili from the diner down the street. If she wasn't willing or able to give him anything, he would threaten her or sit in the corner of the store and shout obscenities at her customers. On more than one occasion, she was sure Daniel was guilty of breaking the glass in her front door.

Daniel would come into SAME Café and demand food. Most of the time he complained and cursed at us. Each time he came in, we would give him the food he ordered and tried our best to explain the concept of community. When we would ask him how he wanted to help, he was never interested. Usually this was fine because it was an opportunity to help, not an obligation. But after so many encounters with him behaving inappropriately and scaring away customers, we were having trouble maintaining a safe community for everyone. We decided something had to change.

We politely reminded him how it worked but predictably, he reacted by yelling at us and threatening violence, even throwing his food back at us. But we held firm to our expectations—we did not tolerate violence or cussing—and for the most part he just avoided the café after that. If he did happen to walk by and make eye contact with us behind the counter, we would catch him flipping us off or shouting a quick insult through the front door. Most of the time we did our best to laugh it off or smile and wave. It was only when there were customers on the patio and he stopped to engage them in a negative way that we felt like we needed to get involved.

This went on for many years. He would sometimes disappear for a while but would eventually pop back up and start the tirade all over again. He was a person who was chronically homeless. No matter how much help he was offered, he was not able to change. His mental illness and alcoholism seemed to have him trapped.

Mental health and alcoholism are not a choice. They take their toll on a person, and for years, he struggled. Daniel was just one of the many people we came across over the years who struggled. Libby and I often talked about how increased mental health care could help a lot of people. It was hard to watch someone struggle with a disease and not have any resources to be able to offer. Even harder still when resources were available and people would not utilize them.

While Herbs and Arts showed us support, some of our other neighbors were not so enthralled that we were bursting at the seams. Seventeen seats are not very many when you are trying to build community and make a dent in food insecurity. We started in a small space because we knew we could handle 600 square feet. But now that the word was out, we were serving more and more customers every day. On good weather days, we would have folks eating on the sidewalk outside because all the tables inside were full. While this wasn't a problem for us, our remaining neighbors were not so thrilled to be having daily picnics happening on the sidewalk in front of their businesses.

Often, these picnickers were a group Libby and I affectionately called "The Kids." The group was made up of a loose circle of creative young folks in their late teens and early twenties. Most of them were artists of some sort—some were musicians, some were sculptors, one was even an artisanal bread maker. Many of The Kids were street performers (we soon learned the proper term is "buskers"). None of them made much money, and so when they found out about SAME Café, it became a regular lunchtime meeting place.

As there were only seventeen seats, if more than a few of the group showed up there wasn't enough seating in the café for everyone. The Kids didn't care—they were happy to go outside and dine on the sidewalk if the weather was nice enough. If it wasn't, Libby and I would look the other way when they took their food downstairs into the basement and ate at folding tables set up in the extra storage space. This was unofficial seating because the fire marshal had not blessed the basement for public occupancy. The fact that it wasn't "allowed" fed into the anarchical nature of The Kids and made them come more often.

Just as they came to support SAME, Libby and I went to many of their musical performances and art shows. It certainly wasn't the mainstream style of artistic expression, but we wanted to show our support as well as expand our horizons and get to know people. At one of these events, Katie and Libby ran into a friend of the café who just happened to have his pet rat in his pocket. Like I said, these kids were unique! Many lasting friendships were born from these excursions outside the café walls. Some of the artists even put together a few fundraising shows for SAME Café.

Oliver was one of our favorites from this group. He started coming in so regularly that we started to keep track. He was determined to win the "title" of most visits to SAME Café in a row. His streak was seventy-seven days. He loved SAME Café so much that he celebrated many birthdays with us, including having a princess themed party. He wanted to have a SAME Café sleep over one night, which Libby reluctantly agreed to, and then (thankfully) everyone bailed at the last minute when sleeping bags started to be laid out on the hard-concrete floor.

One of The Kids decided she wanted to commemorate her love for SAME Café. She had one of her friends tattoo the letters S-A-M-E and C-A-F-E onto her toes. This girl had serious dedication, not to mention pain tolerance. Even I don't have the words SAME Café tattooed on my body.

When October 2007 rolled around, we wanted to celebrate our first anniversary with a party. We knew friends and family would be coming to help us celebrate and needed all the space we could get. We talked our landlord into letting us rent the empty space next door to use for the event. We even had live music. Libby's cousin Jake came all the way from Ohio to play trumpet for the occasion. Aunt Kate and Uncle Phil and our friends who bought the first piece of equipment were able to attend. Lots of regular customers, including many of The Kids, came to the party. The celebration lasted late into the night with a dance party in the basement after all the dishes were finished and the trash taken out.

Harry was a mechanic, a student, an artist and a musician. He fit right in with The Kids, even though he was old enough to be their dad. When he wasn't turning a wrench at a local repair shop or attending classes at Metro State, it was a good bet he'd be spending his lunch hour at SAME. When Harry heard about Oliver's streak, he decided to try and match or break it. He managed to put together a streak of over sixty weekday visits in a row. He didn't beat Oliver, but he gave it a good go.

Harry made a point of coming in for lunch at least two to three times a week since he was still working right around the corner. At first, he came in because of the interesting concept and the convenience, but then he fell in love with the food, friendships and connections. He told me once, "When I'm here it's like I am keeping my finger on the pulse of the neighborhood, and when I can't make it in for a while, I feel like something is missing."

His favorite things to eat were the soups, and he regularly checked the menu online to see which ones were being prepared. If there was a last-minute change or if a particular soup sold out before he was able to make it in for lunch, he would be sure to give us a hard time. He proudly said his palate expanded quite a bit since eating at SAME regularly—especially when it came to leafy greens like chard, kale and arugula.

Harry loved sitting in the front window of the café and watching someone completely new walk in to SAME. He said, "It's always positive, and watching the smiles break out as they take in the concept. It is one of my favorite things." Harry never ate alone intentionally. He was always that guy who would invite someone to sit with him. Often, Harry and Oliver would sit and eat together. They would get so involved in conversation about art or music or the neighborhood that we'd close the restaurant around them before they even noticed the time of day.

So many friendships were being made over meals that were shared. In an atmosphere where so many restaurants fail in their first year, it was a big deal SAME had made it past that milestone. When it first opened, we had the idea that if SAME served a meal to just one person who needed it, then it could be counted as a success. When the numbers were finally tallied, we found in SAME Café's first complete year of operation it served just under 7,000 meals.

"When are we going to go to a baseball game again?" This was usually how we were greeted by Angelo when he walked through the door. Angelo was scheduled to volunteer on Tuesday mornings from 10-11. We called this time slot the "Power Hour" because it was the final rush before we opened for lunch. Angelo would come with his job coach, and the two of them would make sure the dining room was all ready for customers.

Angelo was in his late fifties and volunteered on Tuesdays with us for years. He is developmentally delayed and lives in his parents' basement on Denver's West side. Angelo loves Denver sports, especially the Broncos and Rockies. He used to work at Coors Field where the Rockies play. His favorite past times are listening to tapes on his Walkman and watching *C.H.I.P.s* reruns on TV.

Occasionally, we would take Angelo for an outing on the days when his job coach wasn't scheduled to work with him and when we could get away from the café. We took field trips with him to Hammonds Candy Factory, Red Rocks Amphitheater and even a Rockies game.

Whenever Angelo came in, he would work for an hour rolling silverware, wiping tables and setting out the patio furniture. Once 11:00 rolled around and he flipped the open sign, he would come up and order his lunch. He used to order soup, salad, and two slices of pizza every time he came. He ordered a beet soup once he didn't like so that ended his soup ordering days. Later, his doctor told him he needed to eat healthier and so he stopped ordering two slices of pizza. Even though he volunteered, he would usually take two dollars out of his wallet and put them in the donation box. His smile was infectious, and he always gave great hugs. He loved knowing everyone who was working in the café by name and saying hello to each one of them before he began work.

Chapter 8

Expansion

During the second year we saw quite an increase in the number of customers. Numbers were especially high towards the end of the month when funds started to run short for many people. The café was gaining a bit of notoriety in the neighborhood as a place where anyone could get a healthy, delicious meal. Customers across the entire economic spectrum were coming in for lunch and bringing their friends with them.

The national press coverage certainly didn't hurt either, as SAME Café was a bit of a destination experience. It was so surreal to meet someone from out of state who had driven straight from the airport to the café to have lunch.

Things were getting so busy that days flew by in a bit of a blur. We were figuring out how to run a restaurant, answering phone calls and emails, and doing interviews. It became clear it was time for me to stop splitting my time between the consulting gig and SAME. The needs of the café were becoming too demanding to keep working both jobs. I was more than ready to quit consulting so I could totally focus on the café.

We took the idea of me becoming an actual paid employee to the board of directors. Since the board had been wise enough to pay back the loan initially invested, there were funds that could be allocated for an employee. They agreed to approve a small salary. It would be a huge pay cut, but one we were willing to take. Luckily, Libby was still teaching, so we had the safety net of her salary and health insurance coverage.

Being open for longer hours on the weekend wasn't bringing in nearly as many customers as we had hoped. Even on those longer days, most of the meals were served right during lunchtime. It didn't seem to make sense to continue working an extra six hours to serve so few meals. Many of the customers who came in for lunch sober returned in the evening intoxicated.

At the same time, we were learning from our regulars many of the resource organizations who provided food around the area were closed Sunday and Monday. We proposed to the board of directors that we change the hours of operation to include Mondays and to drop the Saturday evening service. This turned out to be a great adjustment because it became immediately clear Monday was the busiest day of most weeks. The customers also appreciated there was now a consistent set of hours—11am-2pm, for each day the café was open. It's amazing what a difference it can make when you actually listen instead of making assumptions about what people need.

The change in hours was good for us too because it meant we no longer had to work in the café during weekend nights. It was already taking a toll on us working so many hours and burning the candle on both ends. We were so lucky to have great volunteers and friends to help shoulder some of the burden. If our friends weren't washing dishes in the kitchen (hopefully without flooding it!), they were coming in to have lunch or play games with us when it was slow. These friends and many other volunteers were so helpful in holding down the fort. Thanks to the time and energy of friends and dedicated volunteers we were able to survive.

One Saturday afternoon when I was exhausted from a long week, I shuffled outside to lock up the patio chairs and tables. A man approached me and explained he just heard about SAME Café. He wondered if I could help him with a problem. This is usually where someone asks me for the leftovers or some spare change so he can get on the bus (a.k.a. some beer money). I have conditioned myself to never give anyone money no matter how sad the story. I have seen firsthand it's not helpful. Jose introduced himself and went on to share he is homeless. I thought to myself,

"Here it comes," but instead of asking for money, he asked if I could help him get a new pair of boots. His boots got wet the other night in the rain and now they didn't fit him the same. They were tight and rubbing his feet. Jose proceeded to take off his boots and socks right there on Colfax to show me the problem. His feet were in bad shape. He had been walking most of the day and was in pain.

This is not something I normally do but I thought, "O.k. at least he isn't asking for money." I told him if he returned on Monday to volunteer, we'd talk about the boots. He assured me he was not lazy and was a hard worker, and he'd be the best helper he could, even though his feet were hurting him. He explained he'd clean the bathroom, do dishes, take out the trash, whatever. To be honest, I didn't know if he was going to show up on Monday at 10am to volunteer or not.

When I arrived at SAME at 9:30 on Monday with my arms full of groceries, there was Jose, waiting on the patio. He came running in to help when I unlocked the door and continued to work diligently at the dish station all day. He would not even take a lunch break. I had to force him to sit down and eat. He showed up again on Tuesday and Wednesday. He worked harder than most employees would have. When he finished a task, he asked about another. "What else can I do to help?" "How else can I help?" I was so impressed with him. I went out on Wednesday night and bought him the boots. I brought them with me to the café on Thursday. He showed up on time and was so excited that he would get his boots that day.

With his new boots in hand, Jose got in line to grab some lunch. Behind him in line, a man called out his name. He turned around and came face to face with another of our regulars, who happened to be a friend of his. They embraced and were excited to see each other. Immediately, he told his friend how we helped him get the boots. Jose's friend, who donates what he can for his lunch when he has the funds, pulled me aside and asked if he could contribute some money to Jose's boots. He was so moved and grateful we were helping his friend, and he wanted to help, too. I could not believe it. The friend swiped his credit card and donated $10 toward the new pair of boots. Jose walked out of there that day with the greatest smile.

In the fall of 2007, I got a call from a teacher who asked if we were interested in having an intern in the kitchen. We hadn't had an intern before, but the idea of some regular help sounded great since the café was starting to get busier. Especially if the internship was unpaid. We agreed to have a student come twice a week during the lunch shift. We got lucky with the student who was assigned to come. Juan was a quiet young man, but very eager to learn about working in a space that was a non-profit as well as a commercial kitchen. I immediately knew I would enjoy working with him. I loved teaching Juan all about the various parts of running the café. Because we didn't have a lot of help, he got to do some of everything, not just the crap jobs most interns get. He and I would quietly work alongside each other. He would eagerly complete whatever tasks I assigned to him. I remember the first time I asked him to make pizza dough. He was super nervous about screwing it up, but I assured him it was just dough. Of course, it came out fine. Although he was a young man of few words, he eventually shared with me he was hoping to be the first in his family to graduate high school and go on to college. Knowing his work ethic after working with him for those months, I had no doubt he would make that dream come true. Juan was the first of a string of interns SAME was able to utilize to help accomplish all the daily tasks the café required.

One of the things that energized us most about working at the café was the amazing people we got to spend time with during those crazy, busy days. It was especially gratifying when young people would come in and get involved. They reminded us of when we were young and spent time volunteering ourselves. Although having youngsters in and around a commercial kitchen can be dangerous and challenging, we made special efforts to identify developmentally appropriate tasks actually helpful to the daily café operation.

Thanks to the extra help from an intern or two along with a growing number of volunteers, I was able to prepare enough food to keep up with the growing crowds of customers coming to dine at the café. However, space for people to sit was still an issue. During the warmer days, it was possible for customers to take food outside to dine on the newly installed patio, but those days were quickly running out as that summer of 2008 turned to fall.

Eventually, our board of directors decided to bite the bullet and sign a lease on the empty space next door where we had hosted our first anniversary party. A contractor was hired, and the remodeling work began. The plan seemed daunting, but we were glad the board invested the money to put someone else in charge of the construction this time so Libby and I could focus on the daily operation of the café.

The contractor built a handicapped accessible bathroom in the new space, which was a huge upgrade from the cramped closet of a washroom all had to share previously. They also cut a seven-foot hole in the wall to connect the two units together. The goal was to make it feel like a single connected space with a natural flow throughout. When the work was finished, we moved the new chairs and tables to the new dining area and rearranged the kitchen to be larger and more functional.

The project cost right around $15,000 in all, which was quite an investment for a small organization. It took a big chunk out of savings, but we knew the extra space would be well worth it. Heck, the bathroom upgrade alone was a dramatic enough improvement to justify the cost. Adding to that, the new dining room had seating for forty-five customers, and the patio outside doubled in size as well.

We knew an upgrade like that was risky, but thought it was the right decision. That thought was confirmed when friends from the foundation that had purchased the truck the year before walked through the door and magically handed us a check for $15,000. They knew about the expansion, but they had no way of knowing their check almost exactly matched what the contractor had charged. It was just another one of those little miracles provided by the universe that kept us motivated.

SAME celebrated two years in business with a party in the new space just after Thanksgiving when all the construction was complete. We had city council members show up in addition to friends and family. One highlight from the celebration was when a man stopped in to ask if this was the place where a homeless guy could get a meal. I told him about the concept, and he asked if he could make a donation. To my surprise and amazement, he reached in his wallet and pulled out a one-hundred-dollar bill. He explained he wasn't giving Christmas gifts this year and was donating to charities instead. He then asked for the quickest way to walk to the downtown mission, so he could find a bed for the night.

We got to know Lily through her mom, Jenny. Jenny came to us through her job at a small agency that helped children and adults with disabilities. Each week, Jenny would bring a group of four to five adults in on Tuesday morning, and they would help us set up for the day. On a few of those days, Jenny would bring her daughter, Lily, along with her. Lily was only four or five years old when she started coming to help. Lily would ask for a pitcher of water and proceed to water the plants. She loved to fill the salt and pepper shakers and make art for the walls.

Lily must have been around six years old when she asked to be the featured artist for the month. She and Jenny came in and hung about twenty pieces of her original work on the wall. Lily was so excited to see her artwork on display, and they invited friends and family to the art opening reception.

On numerous occasions, Lily would host fundraisers for other non-profits at SAME Café, and still does. She and her mom would make lemonade and hot chocolate, hosting stands outside of SAME Café, donating the proceeds to The Gathering Place—a day shelter for women and children in our neighborhood. Lily loves being at SAME Café and meeting so many different people. She is profoundly caring and sees the world through a different lens than most kids.

Will was about the same age as Lily when he started volunteering. He would come on Friday afternoons and help close the café. He would sweep and mop, take out the trash, clean the tables, water plants and fill salt and pepper shakers. He and his mom or dad would show up every Friday afternoon. I remember asking how they found us, and Will's mom told us one day they were driving down the street and saw a person flying a sign that read "Anything helps." Will asked his mom to give the person some money. Even though he was about five at the time, Will had profound questions for her. He was fixated on doing something. Will's mom promised him she would find an organization where he could volunteer.

On one of his first visits to SAME, Will brought in a baggie full of change and small bills and dumped it in the donation box. He explained that at home when he gets money for chores or birthdays, he gets to spend a third, save a third, and give third of it away. He chose SAME Café to receive the donation that time around. We were so touched by this little guy's generous heart. Will and his family continued volunteering for years and we even made dinosaur shaped sugar cookies for his birthday party one year. It is kids like these who are going to grow up and change the world.

Winter 1999 - Tuesday Night Crew at the Peoria
Rescue Mission

February 2002 - The infamous
inflight magazine page full of
brainstorming notes

June 2006 - The interior of the café before
we started renovating

June 2006 –Libby's sister Katie and I on the
other end of the credenza as it was stuck in the
door. This is the day we met Patty!

October 2006 - The café as it
looked for the first 2 years

October 2006 – Libby and I posing with One
World Café founder, Denise Cerreta, soon
after opening

November 2006 - Uncle Phil's cranes
hanging from the café ceiling

January 2007 – Libby and I posing with Kidd
just before he left for New Orleans

September 2007 – Loading up the "kidnapper van" with supplies

October 2007 – Bob taking a break from doing the dishes

January 2008 – Making pizzas with Libby and Patrick

March 2008 – Libby's friends from her teaching days often came to volunteer

July 2008 – Libby and I at the serving counter

August 2008 – Oliver on the patio in
front of the café

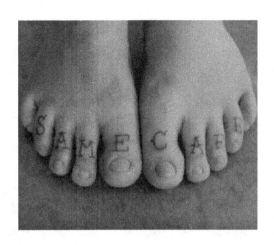

August 2008 – The tattooed toes of one of
The Kids

A local artist drew this picture of the café
for us – it is one of our favorite things

October 2008 – Laughing with customers made
the time fly!

June 2009 - Aussie John in front of
the beverage station

June 2010 – Lily loved to get involved
with neighborhood causes

July 2010 – Baby Nora getting to try her first bite
of one of Libby's famous cookies

September 2011 - Will poses by a pumpkin
almost as big as he was when he first started
volunteering

October 2012 - Mary was so excited to see the cake from our friends at Mulberries Cake Shop when she returned from a trip to Central America

Summer 2012 – The new kitchen
after it was renovated for us by
RFMA

Summer 2012 - The newly updated dining room
after the RFMA renovation

August 2014 – Showing off my new ink. The Latin words mean "Every man a man" Or in other words – we are all the same

September 2015 - Working at my favorite station - serving up slices of pizza

August 2016 - Making soup from a medley of summer squash from the Denver Botanic Gardens

Summer 2017 - Hand painted plates on the wall, made by a local high school art class

Chapter 9

Importance of Connection

When it was all said and done, the total number of customers served in the second year came up to just under 10,000. This was a 30% increase over the first year, not just in the number of people we saw each day but also in the amount of food we had to purchase and prepare. Stopping at the local grocery store each morning was getting to be expensive. When we found the parents of one of our young interns happened to run an organic bulk foods distribution company, we were thrilled. We were finally able to buy staple items—oils, nuts, flour, sugar, etc. —at wholesale prices.

Around this same time a local farmer found us. She was a gardener who had two large urban plots where she grew the greatest vegetables. One day she came walking into the café, covered with earth and wearing a big sun hat, and asked if we'd be interested in purchasing seasonal veggies from her. This was incredible because we had been trying so hard to make connections to local farms. From that day on, each week she'd email a list of what was growing and then she would harvest what we selected and bring it on over. Her vegetables were amazing, plucked from the ground that morning and bursting with beauty and flavor. It didn't matter what the vegetable was, we always said yes to anything she grew, knowing they were going to make the most delicious dishes.

It was a transition having our customers sit and eat in the new dining room. We were used to having conversations with everyone while we were working. Up until that point, diners ate just outside of our open kitchen, and we could visit with them as we prepped veggies and pizzas. Now that customers sat in the dining room, we had less opportunity to interact with them. Most of the conversations were limited to the front counter. We tried to get into the dining room as often as we could, but leaving the kitchen was a challenge. There were still a couple of tables on the kitchen side, and most of the regulars would park there to have their lunch so we could chat.

Alvin was a large Native American gentleman, somewhere in his sixties. Libby had a soft spot for this self-described drunk. He was always wearing a baseball cap with his long, brown hair hanging out the back. He was so intoxicated most of the time that the name I heard slur out of his mouth was Alfred. So for the longest time, that is what we called him. It wasn't until he came in on a rare sober day when we realized our mistake.

Alvin had a bad foot, and the story of how it was injured changed often. Years of living on the streets compounded the issue, and it constantly needed medical attention. He usually drooled into his soup because he often fell asleep at the table, but this gentleman was so kind, nice and appreciative. He always helped or put money in the box. On his worst days, we'd ask him to come back when he was sober and gave him a granola bar or a slice of pizza to go, and he would graciously comply.

We would always have the greatest conversations with Alvin. It was clear he deeply valued the mission of SAME Café, even in his inebriated state. He would bring his companions along with him each day. He had the greatest smile and would somehow talk his way in the door, especially on the coldest days. He never caused a problem. His friends, on the other hand, were a little more challenging. Alvin never yelled or cussed me out, as many others did.

Occasionally, he would say he was getting out of the street life, but things would always get in the way. He had family somewhere. He talked about them a lot, but we never saw any of them, except for his street family. He introduced everyone he brought in as his brother or sister.

One day, Alvin just disappeared and we didn't see him for months. We worried about him and inquired with some of his friends who still came in. No one seemed to know where he had ended up. When he finally reemerged, he was a blur past the front window on a ten speed. Both Libby and I saw him buzz by and turned to each other with looks of puzzlement. "Was that Alfred?" We both said at the exact same time, so shocked at the sight of him that we reverted back to our old name for him. "No, it couldn't be. Alvin could never ride a bike with that foot."

A few days later, Alvin stopped his bike out front when we were sweeping leaves off the patio. He was clean, sober and in permanent housing. He had his foot operated on and was RIDING A BIKE! He hugged us both and chatted with us briefly about his new life. He didn't want to screw it up, so he had to keep moving if he was going to make it to his next appointment on time. Alvin would continue to visit after that but never stayed long. He would stop in to say "Hello" and fill his bike water bottle with water and ice when he was in the neighborhood. On every trip down Colfax, he waved.

When we got busy, sometimes we would just forget about that space and wouldn't go over there very often. Soon, it was evident that was a problem. We weren't having as many genuine conversations with customers. Sometimes, a regular would peak their head around the corner and let us know something wasn't quite right in the dining room. One time someone was filling up their entire thermos with all the coffee. On more than one occasion someone emptied the entire container of sugar packets into their backpack. A few times we'd find patrons sleeping at a back table. The new bathroom was defiled in many ways (sex, drugs, graffiti and things being flushed that shouldn't have). Each time one of these things happened, we would brainstorm what was going wrong and how to fix it. The last straw was when a customer propositioned a female volunteer. Was it all because there was now a permanent wall dividing us? Was it the number of people we were serving? Or was it because we weren't focusing on relationships? We began making a more concentrated effort to build community to see if that would help.

We knew conversation was so important to making this thing work. When Libby was there every day during the summer of 2009, it allowed her to talk to customers more. She would sometimes take her laptop and set up shop in the dining room instead of going to the basement to work. If she was needed in the kitchen, she would hop up and help out. Sometimes, we would ask a regular, highly trusted volunteer to hang out in the dining room, chatting and checking in with guests. We wanted to be intentional about community building and the new kitchen forced us to be creative about how to do that.

This also meant we needed to encourage our regular volunteers to select tables in the dining room to have their lunch. They wanted to stay close to the kitchen and help out if needed or just continue to chat with the other volunteers on their shift. We encouraged them to meet new people and make new friends by eating in the dining room instead of at the few tables left on the kitchen side. We constantly introduced people to one another and encouraged people to share tables with someone they had never dined with before. We did not want to police the dining room. We wanted to facilitate connection.

Not long after our expansion, we got the news a cake shop was moving into the recently vacated tanning salon space. It was a shop we weren't familiar with but had heard good things from customers and friends who had visited their previous location. Knowing they were moving into our block was exciting. Who wouldn't want to work next door to a bakery?

Mulberries Cake Shop was a family run operation—owned by Kip and Kathleen Karr. Kathleen's mom and sister both worked in the store, and their adorable kids would even come in and help on weekends and after school. The Karrs quickly became close friends and amazing supporters of SAME Café. They and their staff often came over to grab lunch throughout the week, and they were always willing to donate delicious baked goods—cakes, cookies, cupcakes —for any of our events without question.

One year on my birthday, Kathleen and the Mulberries crew walked in the front door and surprised me with a cake. Then they made me follow them to the back parking lot where I saw they had also decorated our beloved pickup truck with toilet paper streamers and dozens of balloons.

Having another food related business close by was handy. If we were low on eggs or flour, we knew we could count on Mulberries to have more than enough to share. Kathleen also knew she could borrow extra oven space from SAME whenever they were running short. More than once, the two businesses combined their resources to order bulk ingredients at a discount.

We were lucky to be surrounded by such loving people. They embraced SAME Café's mission and treated us like family. They were the greatest neighbors and are some of the best human beings you will ever meet.

We were a favorite spot for retired folks to volunteer, like Carol and many others. They were excited to be of service and loved working in a commercial kitchen. Some of them were so dedicated to the café that they came once a week, every week for years. They'd share stories and recipes with me and were not shy about suggesting ways to improve the processes around SAME. When Libby was in the café and taking charge, some of the ladies had an adjustment period. They had to get used to a new boss who ran the kitchen in a little more detail-oriented and structured manner (a huge understatement) than I did. While this organization and structure was certainly necessary for our growing establishment, the ladies had a lot to say about it. One of them even asked if I could fire Libby before they realized we were married. (I don't know how they missed that one!) These retirees were such amazing helpers and such hard workers. They were also amazing cooks. I learned a lot of great recipes from working alongside of them.

Carol was one of those special and amazing volunteers. Her nick name was "God's Girlfriend."

—

She brought a smile to my face every time I saw her. She loved schmoozing the customers in the dining room, serving up heaping plates of food. We would remind her we serve in smaller portions to eliminate food waste. Customers could always come back and get more soup and salad. She would respond with, "Just in case this is their only meal for the day," and wink at me. Carol was one of those regular volunteers who would come in grinning and get right to work. She'd do anything we asked; she even loved cleaning the pantry.

Carol was featured in a couple of the videos made about SAME. Her face was even in a few of the news pieces. She insisted on bringing her own bright red, frilly apron when she came to volunteer even though we provided SAME Café aprons for volunteers. She was an incredible listener and friend to anyone at the café. Carol spent most of her life in the elementary education world—maybe that is why she and Libby got along so well.

Carol made many friends while working at SAME. Some of them would come in and ask for her by name. She would sit for hours and listen to those who had very few connections in the world. When Carol was diagnosed with cancer, she couldn't volunteer as much, but she always stopped in and said hello.

One of those friends came by regularly to ask about Carol. He was worried about her and why she hadn't been around as much. When we got the news Carol had passed away, we knew we had to get word out to her friend. The beautiful part about those who lived on the streets around SAME Café was they all looked out for each other. We asked a couple of our regulars to spread the word that we needed to talk to him. Within hours, Shawn walked through the door. With many tears we hugged and told stories about how Carol was so great. He shared with me the small, silver, pocket angel coin Carol gave him long ago. He wore it on a cord around his neck. He said he took "God's Girlfriend" with him wherever he went.

When she passed away, all of us felt a sense of grief. We lost not only a great volunteer but an amazing friend.

A few months later, Shawn was a victim of a hit and run accident. Before the newspapers could even print who the victim was, his friends came and told us of the tragedy. We wept that day for him but found some comfort in the thought that maybe he and Carol were able to reunite their friendship once again.

Chapter 10

An Idea Spreads

We would often share how the press was a double-edged sword. SAME Café needed the press coverage to survive. It was important to get the word out to more folks, but it bothered us that something as essential as building community with our neighbors was making headlines. This was in the day and age before the feel good stories of major news outlets were a thing. Now, almost every media outlet has a forum for getting good news out to the world. Back then, however, we were concerned about sensationalizing sensitive issues for the real people who walked through our doors.

One of the media outlets that caught on to telling good news was *NBC Nightly News with Brian Williams*. I remember reading somewhere his wife inspired the "Making a Difference" segment. She was saying how there are good people out there in the world and they should share those stories in addition to all the bad news they share all the time. So he did. NBC started to send crews to highlight good work and the response was incredible. At the time, Brian Williams had about 11

—
129

million viewers. The impact this segment had on so many folks doing good around the country was enormous from the start.

SAME Café was lucky enough to be featured as one of the first stories in the now famous "Making a Difference" portion of the show in March of 2009. The producers warned us to be ready for the response after the show aired, but we had no idea what to expect.

We watched the show from the basement of the café on a TV borrowed from a customer. A few of us gathered around the tiny TV, some of our closest friends and board members. It was a beautiful segment, about three minutes long, that eloquently shared the story. As soon as the piece ended, the phone started ringing non-stop. People who had seen the show were calling because they wanted to know more about the concept, to share their response, and some even wanted to know where they could send donations. In all, there was an overwhelming number of phone calls and emails and around $10,000 in donations because of that one single broadcast.

Perhaps even more significant than the immediate response was the long-lasting impact that came from individuals who happened to be watching the news that evening. Several people became regular, long-distance contributors to the café who still to this day have never stepped foot inside the space. Many viewers became customers for the first time, some of them driving long hours to include SAME in their road trips.

We later found out Ron Schaich, then CEO of Panera Bread Company, had been watching and decided that evening to propose to his board that Panera should change the format of some of their existing restaurants to mirror what SAME Café was doing. Apparently, the reaction from the board was mixed, but he was able to convince them to take a chance with one of their locations in St. Louis, Missouri. Their pilot project was a success, so they expanded the experiment and opened Panera Cares restaurants in five other cities around the country.

In another part of the country, music legend Jon Bon Jovi was home watching the news with his wife, Dorothea. The power couple had long been using their resources and influence in the New Jersey town of Red Bank to help folks experiencing hunger, poverty and homelessness. Now they had seen another concept that intrigued them. Before long, we received a phone call from the JBJ Soul Foundation asking lots of questions and finally setting up a site visit so they could experience the café in person. They eventually opened a restaurant called Soul Kitchen in Red Bank. Their set up was quite a bit different from that of SAME Café, but they still focused on getting quality meals to people who need them the most. No other single café has brought such a large amount of credibility and notoriety to the community café movement. Since then, the foundation has opened two more Soul Kitchen restaurants in other New Jersey towns.

The response to this press coverage meant a lot of new customers streaming through the café doors. In addition to the customer increase, the amount of work in the office became overwhelming. After much discussion, it was decided Libby needed to stop teaching so she could be at the café full-time. It was either have her come on full-time, or we were going to have to hire someone else. This was a difficult decision for her mainly because she loved her teaching job, and the school was so supportive of the work we were doing. It eventually became evident she was only able to give the children in her classroom 50% of her energy and attention and that did not sit well with her. She wanted to give 100% but just couldn't with the demands of the café.

Once she was no longer torn by her commitment to teaching, Libby began to put all her efforts into SAME. We found that we were both spending upwards of eighty hours a week working. Not all those hours were behind the counter, cooking and serving guests. Some of those hours were spent out around town, attending events with like-minded organizations spreading the word about SAME Café.

Mary was a co-worker of Libby's from school and willing to help us have some time off. When Mary offered to come in on Saturdays, we jumped at the opportunity. She was the perfect person to help.

She had a great temperament and everybody loved her. We hired and trained her to run the front and organize volunteers so we could have some Saturdays off together. She was our first actual employee, a thought that really freaked us out. Now, we had someone else depending on us and we didn't have an employee manual or anything like that.

We were so grateful to have some time to recharge, knowing she was engaging everyone who walked through the door and surrounding them with love. Mary met Carol while working at the café. They were both teachers and loved to travel. They bonded immediately and became fast friends. Like Carol, Mary was treasured by everyone who came in. Her heart was true, and she valued every relationship she built through the café. I remember one of the news outlets interviewing her. She said, "I don't have to talk about how the world could be or should be. I just get to be part of it every day and see this is what the world is." We would have never survived those years without Mary's help.

We started hearing from folks all over the country who wanted to open community cafés. We often found ourselves spending hours on the phone with people, answering questions about SAME. One couple in California already had a non-profit and wanted to expand their mission. Another couple with a café in Spokane, Washington contacted us about changing to the pay-what-you-can model. Ideas were popping up in the minds of people all over, and we were often the first people they called. It was exciting and exhausting. We always encouraged those who inquired about the model to spend as much time as possible in our space. This way, we could get to know the café dreamers and help them more effectively. The questions they asked were more relevant when they'd seen it and lived it for a day or two or more, just as our idea came into focus after our road trip to visit One World Café in Salt Lake City. We knew the power of physically being in the space and seeing it in action. We also encouraged folks to contact Denise and her One World Café crew so they could gain from their experience and perspective as well.

This type of restaurant is so complex. You are not just serving food. Some days you are a social worker, a friend, a nurse, an accountant, a chef, a custodian, a father and at times a bouncer, all before you are even open for the day. Nothing is better than firsthand experience. While working alongside people, you begin to see which ones will likely be capable of juggling the different hats and putting in the hours of hard work to make a café happen. We were excited and spent tons of time and energy cheerleading these efforts and all the inquiries that rolled in.

Two groups came forward from the Denver Metro area and wanted to pick our brains about starting more community cafés in our neck of the woods. There was Cathy Clements who started her conversation by asking if she could open a branch of SAME Café in a nearby suburb. Then there was a group of ladies about retirement age who called themselves the "Three Old Broads." They were determined to have a community café in the very hip and trendy neighborhood of the Highlands.

Cathy originally wanted to provide transitional housing in the Englewood area, which is about five miles south of downtown Denver. But then she fell in love with the SAME Café model over lunch one day. We were personally stretched at first when Cathy approached us. We certainly wanted everyone to have access to healthy food, but we weren't ready to branch out to a second location. It was also hard to share all our "secrets." We had worked so hard for so many hours creating menus, policies and procedures that sharing was not the easiest at first.

Libby regretfully remembers a time when she broke down crying when Cathy asked for some document it had taken Libby hours to create. At one point, when she could finally articulate why that was so hard for her, she shared, "It's not that I was afraid of competition, but to be honest, I was jealous. Jealous that these new cafés would not have to struggle like we did." After Libby reflected on her self-described selfish reaction to Cathy's request, she invited them to come to the café and be in the space as much as possible. Libby said, "I just had to be reminded that by doing what you love, you inspire and awaken the hearts of others." Cathy and her team's hearts were awakened. They volunteered even after they opened Café 180. They continue to learn, grow and share ideas with us.

Mentoring them through the process of opening was one of the most challenging and rewarding things we did up to that point. We saw the impact of sharing and being generous with other likeminded individuals. It became clear to us sharing meant so many more people could be touched by this model. We are proud to say Café 180 is still operating at the time of this publication. Their non-profit has expanded beyond the community café model to include their original goal of housing. They even provide counseling and a job training program through an E-bike store.

The Three Old Broads took a slightly different approach. In 2010, they opened Comfort Café, a place where folks who were grieving could share recipes and meals together. This unique twist would be combined with the pay-what-you-can model. They took a risk on a space in a trendy neighborhood northeast of downtown. A couple of the founders volunteered once or twice at

SAME Café before they opened. After those few volunteer experiences, we heard very little from them.

Comfort Café closed after two years in business. While they were an entirely independent operation, this was a challenge for us. It was hard to see a café close and even harder for the broader public to grasp. People would call or stop in and ask why we closed Comfort Café? We would have to respond that although we were cheerleaders for their work, that café was not part of SAME. It also gave us pause and made us think about how to ensure SAME Café could survive. We had to wonder, why did they close? Was it their location? The complex model combining grief with pay-what-you-can? What challenges did they face that we could avoid and help others avoid in the future?

As many more groups came to us and asked for help, we did our best to give them sound advice. We spent countless hours on conference calls and made road trips to potential locations. We attended meetings in person and via Skype to lend support and advice to these new cafés in hopes they could open and be successful. With the help of Denise Cerreta and her newfound organization, One World Everybody Eats, we were excited to see the concept expand.

Denise organized and scheduled a yearly gathering of like-minded people who were all interested or already invested in the community café idea. It was always a great weekend of sharing ideas and challenges. We loved hearing the updates from open cafés. It was also fun to hear about which city was working on creating the next community café. This yearly gathering was a time for Libby and I to connect to others who were doing the same thing and who understood the unique challenges of running a café. Being the longest running café in the network (One World Café in Salt Lake City eventually closed), we often shared more than we learned. The relationships were more important to us than the content at these events.

Another person who saved us time and again was Jay. Jay was a former call center coordinator for a telecom company, and he had recently left his job. He found himself wanting to get involved with an organization mainly to get out of the house. On a suggestion from his partner, he came in to check out the crazy café on Colfax that had been recently featured on the news. He wandered in on a Friday and we all hit it off. He had such great energy. We could always count on a boost in kitchen moral whenever he came in and started telling stories or occasional bad jokes.

Jay was willing to help however he could. As we got to know him better, we found him to be extremely valuable. He and Mary often tag teamed when we needed a day off and they would run the restaurant to give us a break.

I'll never forget the time Jay watched the café for us when Libby and I both needed to leave town for a family event. Before we left, we stocked the refrigerator with an entire weekend's worth of soups and salads so all he would have to do each morning was some easy prep work. Jay had been volunteering at the café for so long we knew we were leaving it in good hands.

When the phone rang early that Saturday morning and we saw Jay's number, our pulses skyrocketed. He informed us the refrigerator had failed overnight and all the food we had prepared was completely ruined. There we were hundreds of miles away with a minor crisis brewing at the café, and there wasn't a darn thing we could do about it. We suggested that they hang a note on the door, "Café closed due to an emergency," and we would deal with the mess when we returned in a few days. But Jay didn't want to accept defeat. He and the other volunteers discarded the spoiled food, made replacement dishes and were ready to open by 11am.

Jay was not only a natural fit in the kitchen, but he also had the business expertise to help us when it came time to work on the budget and write grants. When the board of directors had an opening, we looked immediately to Jay and asked if he would be willing to apply. He ended up serving on the board for a couple of years until it came time for him and his partner to move back to the Chicago area to take care of his aging parents.

In 2011, Libby was nominated to give a TEDx Mile High talk. She had to go through a series of interviews to be selected. She worked for so long writing and practicing the speech entitled "Dignity, Community and a Side of Veggies." The TEDx team had her practice so many times, giving her pointers on how to memorize the speech and deliver it well. She sent draft after draft to the team, each time focusing in on what stories to share and how to make the most impact with those seven precious minutes. They were very serious about keeping it to seven minutes.

"Those dress rehearsals scared me to death!" Libby recalls. "I could barely get through the speech without messing up. Being on that stage, I was nauseous. I had never spoken in front of that many people before!" The TEDx event was being held at the Ellie Caulkins Opera House, which can hold over 2,000 people. It was completely sold out.

On the day of the presentation, she was so nervous. Once it was her turn, she delivered an amazing talk not just about SAME Café but about human dignity. When she returned to her seat, amidst the first standing ovation of the night, she fell onto my shoulder exhausted. Libby shared, "I don't know if I had ever been so relieved that something was over."

At the break, we were able to mingle with folks from the audience who were clamoring to know more about SAME. One of them shared with us how cute it was to watch her return to her seat and lean on me. They were all wanting to volunteer, donate, and get involved. We were overwhelmed by the response. So many people signed up to volunteer or came in to have lunch. Each time saying, "I heard your Ted Talk."

Bonnie found herself on East Colfax one afternoon during a pretty bad snowstorm. She saw the sign for SAME Café and it jogged something in her memory. She had read about SAME years earlier in one of the newspaper articles. She was interested in the concept but had not yet made the time to come over. She looked in the windows and realized the snowstorm was so bad that the café wasn't open, but she resolved to come back again.

The next time Bonnie came, she asked to speak with the person in charge of volunteering and was directed to Libby. She told Libby she was planning to come back on Saturday and all she wanted to do was wash our dishes. This was really exciting to hear, since usually volunteers are more interested in cooking or serving food. So Libby gave Bonnie a big hug and wrote her name down on the volunteer calendar for Saturday afternoon.

Bonnie showed up as promised that Saturday and many more afterwards. She would walk through the door armed with long rubber gloves, strap on an apron and proudly take her place at the dish sink. By the end of the shift she was usually soaked, sweating and smiling profusely. Bonnie shared with us during our times working together that she was mildly autistic, and she relished jobs that allowed her to focus and see immediate results. She is raising her son, who has a more severe form of Autism. Several times she brought Jake in and they would work at the dish sink together.

Besides the glory of the dish sink, Bonnie also loved to come to SAME because she knew she could find foods on the menu that fit her diet. From time to time, she would find herself on a limited income, and there were very few places she could affordably eat and be assured she was staying true to her chosen vegan lifestyle. We were always glad to accommodate dietary restrictions when possible, and we made sure to make notes of the ingredients of each dish so the server at the front counter could answer dietary questions when they came up.

When SAME's board of directors announced an open employee position, Bonnie was one of the first people who applied. Her application had one caveat; she wanted to come on as an intern rather than a full-blown board member. She wanted the intern role because it would allow her to get her feet wet, to see what the roll was like and give her some flexibility in case the position became too overwhelming for her to fill. However, that was never an issue. Bonnie flourished in her role on the board, eventually transitioning to a full member and even becoming an officer.

Chapter 11

A New Look

One afternoon, after we'd finished cleaning up for the day and were just about to head home, the phone rang. Libby looked at the caller ID and noticed the name was that of a local brew pub and thought, "Why would they be calling us?" We were about to run out the door, but curiosity got the best of her and she answered. She had a very odd conversation with someone who was asking her to describe our kitchen. While on the phone she tried to convey that our kitchen was basic but we made it work. He asked if he could come and tour the space the next morning. Libby jokingly told him, "Sure, it'll take about five minutes!" We agreed to meet this man and give him a tour of the space, not really understanding why he wanted to see it.

Just as promised, Bill showed up the next morning. While touring the kitchen, he shared he was part of a group called Restaurant Facility Management Association (RFMA) and they were looking for a non-profit to help. Because this group had experience and expertise managing the operations of some of the biggest commercial restaurant groups in the country (like Red Lobster and Chipotle) they wanted to help improve an organization where their expertise could be put to good use. The previous year, they had helped a homeless shelter revamp their kitchen so they could serve more people. All the facility managers donated their time and got the companies they worked for to donate materials. They then would spend a week on site making all the changes.

Bill wanted to make SAME his nomination for the award for that year. As he walked out the door, he noticed I was boiling water in an electric skillet to make pasta for a salad. Because we didn't have gas or an electric stove in the space, that is how we had to heat things up to boil. He explained there was a nomination process and we'd have to wait and see but he was certain if we were selected, this process would change our lives.

We were excited right away about the prospect of having professionals renovate our kitchen. We had created the kitchen on a shoe-string budget and did the best we could but knew there was room for major improvements. We were also guarded because this award sounded too good to be true. There had been a few times over the years where someone promised something and they never delivered. This time we tried not to get our hopes up but shared with the board the encounter anyway. We got right back to the everyday tasks of serving soup, salad and pizza and the idea of having a new kitchen floated right out of our minds.

A few months later, Bill called out of the blue and asked if he could bring a group of engineers to the café to evaluate if we were a good fit. "This is a good sign," he told us. The group was moving forward in the selection process. Again, trying to not get too excited, we shared the status with our board of directors. More than one of them commented on their surprise. They thought he'd forgotten all about us.

A couple of weeks later, Bill asked to set up a time when we could have a final interview over the phone with the executive director of RFMA. This meant we were finalists! We cleared our schedules and made a date. He insisted both Libby and I be available at the same time. We made the appointment for 9:00 am and he said he'd see us then. All three of us would need to be on the phone for this final interview.

The morning of the interview arrived. We found Bill waiting outside, and he seemed just as anxious as we were. It was a big deal for him to have the organization he had nominated be selected. He asked us to head down to the office and be by the phone ready to take the call. Right then, the notorious Daniel walked up and demanded my attention. Even though we weren't open, I knew if I didn't take a moment with this challenging customer, we'd pay for it later. He had a history of violent outbursts if he didn't get his way, like throwing a rock through our neighbor's window when she wouldn't buy him lunch. I stepped out the front door to see if I could quickly help him as Libby led Bill inside.

The two of them went immediately downstairs to the office and, of course, the phone rang. Knowing how important the call was, Libby answered right away even though I wasn't in the room yet. I was still upstairs trying to explain to Daniel, who was already drunk, we'd be open at 11am, just like every other day. As I made my way downstairs, I could hear Libby crying. I rushed into the office to hear her say through her tears, "Can you repeat that? Brad just walked in." The person on the phone began to explain again the call was not a final interview but an announcement to let us know SAME had been selected for the RFMA Award for 2012. All three of us jumped up and down and cried tears of joy.

When March of 2012 arrived, it was time for construction to begin. The entire process was unbelievable. It started with consultations from restaurant designers and engineers. We talked about making the space more efficient, increasing refrigeration capacity, moving the drink station, etc. etc. etc. The renovations included installing a ventilation hood, a grease trap and a gas line to the space. At first, we were promised the renovations would only take two to three days. However, there were tons of complications with permits and scheduling conflicts between all the companies involved in RFMA. The café ended up being closed for three weeks. But the final product was amazing and so worth it.

By the time the process was complete, the kitchen was the professional restaurant kitchen of our dreams. It was properly laid out with efficiency in mind. That renovation did change our lives as Bill had predicted. SAME Café had floor drains that didn't overflow every time you let the water out of the sink! We could finally take down those signs and stop warning people about the potential floods as part of their volunteer orientation. There was more workspace, and more pieces of equipment than we thought we would ever use. Ten gallons of stock could be made at one time, and more than three people could be in the kitchen.

Up until this point, Libby and I had been schlepping the laundry home every couple of days and washing the towels and aprons in our washing machine at home. We'd bring each load back to the café, and sometimes it would take a volunteer an hour to untangle the mess that was made by the apron strings in the dryer. Thanks to RFMA, there was now a professional laundry service that provided clean towels and aprons each week at no cost to the café.

Now that we had a sanitizing machine, Libby thought she could relax her vigilance at the dish station. But alas, that did not happen because each volunteer needed to be retrained on how to use the machine properly. Some folks thought the dishes could go into the machine dirty (not true) and others thought they didn't need to use the machine at all (also not true.) But when used correctly, the dish machine was an amazing addition to the café.

Once we were finally back open, customers were excited to see the new space and we were so excited to be building community again. We would be able to boil water—eventually. That ended up taking months to get figured out, as we had to work with the gas company to get gas through the walls of a century-old, three-story cement building.

Eventually, cooking on the gas stove was an absolute luxury compared to what we had been doing before. The soups were faster to prepare and easier. No more putting the veggies to sweat in a soup warmer for an hour before moving on. It was now possible to create rich, complex flavors in a matter of minutes on the stove top. The additional oven space meant there could be one oven dedicated to cookies and one oven to pizzas.

The new equipment also helped us to be more efficient during harvest season. We now had the freezer, oven, and prep space to process so many more vegetables. We could receive more produce at the peak of ripeness and then process and store it for the off-season. This was essential for helping us to keep costs down during the winter months.

The improvements meant SAME was able to serve more customers than ever before. We were able to fit more people into the kitchen effectively and to have great conversations utilizing the new volunteer space. The efficient kitchen design allowed us to establish a rhythm and to focus on relationships. It's like when I'm in the middle of a long distance run and everything feels good. My form feels right, I am drinking enough to stay hydrated, and I'm running at a pace that will allow me to keep going for miles and miles without burning myself out. The rhythm became a groove, and for years we were able to stay in that established routine, building connections.

One of the volunteers Libby featured in the TEDx Mile High presentation was Taryn. Taryn was always willing to do anything to help. She was the ultimate networker—she always brought someone new or was telling someone about SAME. She convinced tons of people to volunteer with us from her tennis connections. One of our early employees, Jil, came to us by way of Taryn. Additionally, a couple of long-standing volunteers and board members found SAME by way of Taryn's network. She was always working out something for SAME. I remember one time talking to Taryn about why she volunteered, and she told me she thought the less fortunate were angels cast to Earth to test the more fortunate. She is one of the most generous hearts you will ever find on this planet.

Taryn's ex-husband was a long-distance runner and when she found out I ran marathons, she wanted to introduce us right away. Mike was always awesome about including me in anything in the running group. He'd invite me to weeknight runs at breweries and run club movie nights. They both showed up to marathons Libby and I were running and cheered us on. Mike even rode his bike for about ten miles next to Libby and I while we ran the Rock N' Roll marathon in Denver.

Once they found out I was trying to qualify for Boston, they were hooked. They would follow my progress at races in person and online, and we had quite a celebration when I finally qualified. They also shared in my devastation when registration for the race opened and amazingly sold out before I could even get to the computer to sign up.

Little did I know that behind the scenes, Taryn and Mike were working every connection they had to see if they could get me a race entry. They would tell everyone they knew I had qualified legitimately but just missed the window of opportunity to register. It was a long shot, but somehow, they pulled it off, probably because of their dedication and Mike's connections in the running community.

They surprised Libby and I in the café—inviting everyone to come and have lunch and be part of the surprise. They wrapped up my framed confirmation letter and a bunch of Boston memorabilia and had me open it in the dining room filled with customers, friends, and family. It was unbelievable—I was going to run the Boston Marathon in 2012 after all! Libby and I both cried. Taryn and Mike even volunteered in the café the week of the race so we both could go to Boston and experience something I had worked so hard for over the last twelve years. It was a dream come true because of their generosity. If it weren't for SAME and the people we met there, I would never have had this life-changing moment.

Chapter 12
Scaling Up

From 2012 – 2016, we were focused on feeding people and building community every day while the café was expanding in more ways than the kitchen. We had more people volunteering and more food coming through the door than ever due to our expanding relationships with local farmers.

Growing Colorado Kids was a group led by Denise Lines. Denise was a former coworker of Libby's from her teaching days. She started GCK to support young refugee children in the processes of growing and preparing fruits and vegetables. When she approached us to ask if we were willing to collaborate with her, we jumped at the chance. They started growing vegetables for SAME which was thrilling for us and them.

Working in people's backyards, since most of the refugee families lived in apartments and had no space for gardens, GCK grew all kinds of things. They even used our back yard for a season to grow. The kids would get so excited about harvesting and seeing what they were able to nurture through the season. The young people would harvest and deliver the goods they had grown, and then work in the kitchen to prepare dishes for the day. They loved when it was time to taste the pizza they made topped with the basil or tomatoes they grew.

There were more jobs to do in the kitchen and we needed help. We took on interns and hired various part-time people to carry some of the load. We eventually bit the bullet and hired some full-time help as well. Each addition brought something new to SAME and helped us grow, both personally and organizationally. With all this growth, came the realization we were not good bosses.

Libby and I had no idea what to do with employees, especially when someone wanted time off or to use their vacation days. Or what to do when someone who was scheduled to work didn't show up. Sometimes systems and internal structure were developed only after an employee would make a suggestion or question something. Our first full-time employee had been working for three months before we realized we did not have an employee manual. We had no idea if she got paid time off because there was no policy for it. Hiring and firing staff was also challenging. It was all new to us. We learned a lot of hard lessons in those days and appreciate every one of those employees.

Part of the problem was Libby and I had the tendency to want to do things ourselves. It wasn't always that I thought I could do it better. I often didn't want to trouble anyone. I also thought it would get done faster if

I did it myself rather than explaining the process to someone else. Even if that person was being paid and the task was within the scope of their job, I would take the easy way out.

Delegation was just not our strong suit. It should have been a warning sign that we were insufficient at delegation when we were working long hours and feeling totally indispensable. Libby often talks about how she was a perfectionist when it came to the café and most other areas of life. She had high expectations for the tasks to be done. Sometimes she wouldn't even trust me to do some of the jobs. Giving up some of the responsibilities was scary for her. She worried constantly someone would let her down.

The problem with doing everything ourselves was we would get constantly caught up in the minutia of the day-to-day operations. That meant the bigger picture tasks of running the organization would get continually pushed to the back burner. It also meant we were the only ones who knew how to do certain things. No one else had keys to the doors, passwords to accounts or codes to the safe. If anything would have happened to us, the organization would have been in trouble.

Looking back now, I wonder if it was a sort of procrastination. We were intimidated by those bigger tasks, so we hid from them by immersing ourselves in the small stuff. It took a while, but we were finally able to break that habit and utilize the people we had on staff to enable us to work on other parts of the business.

One of the areas where we needed a staff member the most was at the front counter. The message each customer heard on their first visit to the café was so important. In those first few moments, they needed to hear how the café worked, what was being served and how they were encouraged to participate. The words used in that initial greeting made a huge impact on someone's experience.

Volunteers were excited about serving and would often want to greet and serve customers. That created some inconsistent messaging which led to some very confused customers. Some well-meaning volunteers would tell people all the food was donated. Some customers were told they were required to pay for their meal. We even overheard one volunteer tell a customer who appeared homeless the food was free. None of these messages were exactly right.

While a very small percentage of the food was donated, most of it was purchased from highly reputable sources. It was important for people to know the dishes were prepared with quality, fresh ingredients, not someone else's leftovers. While there was no set price for the food, saying it was free seemed to tell that customer they had nothing to contribute, they had no value, and thus needed a "free" meal.

Carmen was one of those customers who just couldn't be satisfied. Libby hated to wait on her, and in the early days, she'd switch with someone else so she didn't have to run the front counter when she saw Carmen coming. She always had questions about how things were prepared and complained that she couldn't eat certain things—typically after they were plated. I'd usually have to take the plate back and remake it with the other menu options to satisfy her. She often had a sour look on her face when I would hand her plate across the counter.

Carmen never seemed to be excited to be there. She was a neighborhood resident and always walked over. Often, she would donate some change in the box once she got her cookie—which she usually shared with the dog she walked at lunchtime.

One particular day, Libby was in the back and a volunteer was running the front when Carmen approached and asked if she could speak to the manager. We always got nervous when someone asked that question because it was usually followed by a complaint. Luckily those were few. A feeling of dread came over Libby, making her think, "Crap! What's wrong now?" She moved slowly through the kitchen, praying softly under her breath that this wouldn't be a big deal.

Carmen was surprised when Libby approached her and she said, "You're the manager?" People assume the oldest person, usually a man, behind the counter is the manager. "Yep" was all Libby could reply. Carmen proceeded to share with Libby she was sorry she couldn't donate more on a regular basis and pushed a grocery bag roughly into Libby's hands. Libby carefully looked inside the bag as Carmen walked away.

Inside the crumpled grocery bag were small greeting cards. Carmen had made about 100 cards with stickers and stamps she wanted to donate. Libby was embarrassed and surprised this crotchety customer had made such a sweet gesture.

From that day on, Libby and Carmen became buds. No longer did Libby run from the front when she saw Carmen coming, usually the opposite. This kind gesture opened Libby up to giving Carmen a chance. Through lots of conversations, Libby learned the reason Carmen was so picky about her food was because she had dental issues and couldn't chew most of the menu items. She also learned Carmen had a son in prison whom she visited often and tried to help by making connections with local galleries to hang his artwork, along with that of other prisoners.

She eventually, tearfully, shared with us she had been living with cancer. SAME Café was her connection to healthy food. It wasn't long before her battle with cancer got so hard she could only come to SAME Café on the days she felt strong enough to make the walk over.

Carmen was a good lesson for us (as were many of our toughest customers). She showed us that only through connection and conversation do we really build community. Because she had access to the healthy food she was looking for, Carmen continued to come back around. But what she really needed even more than the food was the connection. Some days she didn't eat that much but she loved just getting out of the house and visiting with people who understood her and knew her well enough not to serve her too many leafy greens that were hard to chew. Carmen is one of those people Libby thanks the universe for. Not only because Carmen helped her to become a better person, but also because her situation helped us realize we needed to train our staff and volunteers to be more compassionate and patient with some of our more challenging customers.

Every customer needed to be given the opportunity to recognize their own inherent dignity. Customers are encouraged to participate, but how and if they do so is completely up to them. The goal is to make sure they understand that every human being, regardless of their station in life, has something valuable to contribute.

To keep the message and wording consistent, we found it necessary to establish a front counter position. This person was the initial point of contact for anyone who entered the café. They were also the one that answered any questions or dealt with any issues customers might have had. This could have been anything from a food complaint to an issue with another patron. This position required extensive training. It was often a staff member who ran the front but eventually we were able to train core volunteers to help in this role.

Adding staff members meant we had to bring in more money to cover the increased payroll. Fundraisers were another one of those necessary aspects of running a non-profit where Libby and I had no experience. Thankfully, the board of directors and many of the volunteers were willing to help make these events possible.

When we first met Kelly and Tyler, they introduced themselves and asked about volunteering. They ate their first meals, Kelly choosing to volunteer to do dishes, and they were hooked. They came back almost every single day. Some days they dropped money in the box, some days they rolled up their sleeves and volunteered for an hour or more. Both were such great helpers and hard workers.

After a couple of weeks working alongside them, Kelly confided they had recently left their hometowns and were living in their car. This alarmed us because they were both so young—they seemed old enough to drive but not yet old enough to drink. Both of them identified as transgender, and they had a hard time feeling safe most places.

We worked side by side with them so often, teaching them basic culinary skills and having great conversations. After a while they felt comfortable asking questions and making some suggestions about different aspects of SAME's operations. We could see how invested they were, how much they seemed to truly care about SAME's success, and we were open to hearing their perspectives. The two of them shared with us that depending on who ran the front, they could be treated differently. Each time they were in line, they would hear the person at the front counter explain the process a little differently, and they realized not everybody got the same spiel.

After one such moment, Kelly took me aside and shared the volunteer who was running the front had accepted a penny from the customer in front of her and didn't ask the customer to help in any other way. She shared how it hurt her feelings, and she felt like that meant the hour she volunteered at SAME was worth one penny. Her perspective was eye opening, and really challenged us to evaluate the way we train volunteers and staff to interact with the guests in a way that acknowledges the dignity in every human being.

Kelly and Tyler eventually used their experience at SAME on their job applications and were able to obtain employment at a local restaurant where they soon became managers. Kelly told us once that SAME Café reminded them they were valuable and capable at a time in their lives when they felt worthless. Kelly loved that SAME Café could find a place for anyone who brought willingness and a good attitude. They loved hearing about the lives of other volunteers who worked alongside them in the café. Kelly and Tyler were fully engaged in the experience of SAME

Café—a place, in their own words, where they could feel normal.

Each summer for ten years SAME had a fund-raising golf tournament, initially organized by Katie and Rich. After they moved away, their local friends Dina and Bill took on the monumental task of coordinating this event. We were grateful for the many friends and family members who would make their way to Denver year after year so they could golf, have fun and help raise some money to support SAME. All of this effort culminated in the biggest fundraiser of the year, often bringing in close to $10,000.

Besides the golf tournament, we held a few other types of fundraising events. We tried our hand at holding a poker tournament for a few years. We also held seasonal banquets, concerts, running races, movie and games nights. While very necessary, fundraising was far from our favorite part of running the café. The events were a lot of work for us, mainly because we had no idea what we were doing. However, they were a lot of fun and a great opportunity to facilitate interactions within the community in ways that weren't possible during normal café operations.

One of the most frequent forms of fundraising was renting out the café space in the evening. Although it required a staff member to be present, sometimes cooking food before and cleaning afterwards, it was a great way to utilize the café during off hours. Groups would come in for meetings, birthday parties, presentations, and even the occasional wedding. Beyond using the space and bringing in extra income, these were awesome opportunities for sharing SAME with people who might not have had the chance to see it otherwise. We were often asked to share the café's story and mission with the groups at some point during those evenings. After hours events also created opportunities for people to volunteer who couldn't find time to do so during regular café operations.

Another way to raise funds was through the grant writing process. Since Libby took on the role of executive director, part of her job was to apply for those grants. She spent countless hours researching which grants were available, which ones SAME Café might qualify for, and filling out all the necessary paperwork. Most often, the grants SAME applied for were from small, local foundations in the immediate area. She never chased after national or government grants, mostly because those types of funds usually required a small organization like SAME to change its entire program just to fit their priorities. They also required a ton of paperwork and record keeping we just didn't have time to do. That was something the organization was not willing to take on just for the sake of some extra dollars.

It took a combination of funding sources to cover the costs necessary to run the café. The money that came in through the donation box only covered about one third of those expenses. Fundraisers and grant writing brought in another third. The remainder of the money needed came from generous, individual donors.

Many times donation checks would come through the mail along with notes explaining how the donor had heard about SAME Café or why they felt motivated to send financial support. Many donors mentioned they wanted to help purchase meals for those in need. Sometimes the gift was in honor of a friend or relative who had passed. Other folks were motivated to donate because they had been through hard times themselves and recognized the importance of spaces like SAME Café.

No matter their motivation, those donations were greatly appreciated. Without the support of the donors, the volunteers and the customers that came to eat each day, SAME Café could not have continued to exist. Organizations like this can only thrive when people come together as one community, share their gifts, and lend support to one another.

Gary was a retired engineer who was looking for a way to get involved in a regular volunteer role. His wife, Mary, happened to be a high school classmate of Libby's parents, and she was aware of SAME Café through that connection and through articles in the *Denver Post*. When Mary found out about the golf tournament and that Libby's parents would be in town, she and Gary signed up to play.

At a potluck before the golf tournament, Gary and Mary were able to reconnect with Libby and many of her family members. They signed up as volunteers on the spot and their first day was a busy and rewarding experience. When they came in the next week, we started to assign tasks for the morning. Gary said he preferred to do dishes. The regular volunteers who made up the rest of the Tuesday crew were very excited about this because they preferred to do anything else.

Almost every Tuesday morning we could count on the dish sink being Gary's domain. He enjoyed five years as the chief dishwasher on the Tuesday morning shift. Just like a good engineer, he had a very precise method for handling each dish as it came back and went through his system. If he was caught up on dishes, Gary would look around and see if there was anything that needed fixing. He was not only great at small repairs but fantastic at sharpening knives and various processing blades in the kitchen.

The first time we asked him to help with some food prep during one of the lulls in dish work, he actually refused. He said he couldn't be trusted to do a good enough job, but Libby was able to convince him to start by just washing and peeling carrots. From then on, we could occasionally convince him to jump in and help with food related tasks, but he would always default to dishes if he had the choice.

Because of Gary's knowledge and willingness to help fix things around SAME, it gave us the courage to try and make some repairs of our own, rather than completely replacing the item or calling in an outside company to make an expensive repair. From refrigerators to ovens to commercial coffee makers, the list of repairs that was accomplished with Gary's help easily saved thousands of dollars.

Chapter 13

Building Community

Building community has its challenges, but it's definitely worth it. At SAME every person who came through the door was an individual with inherent dignity. That translated to giving everyone the same spiel, learning peoples' names, remembering certain things about them, and valuing whatever gifts they contributed. The staff was encouraged to pay attention to how customers responded to previous menus. The person who was running the front counter might have remembered they were likely to avoid the pizza that had olives on it or they wouldn't have wanted the tomato soup because they had an allergy. When someone said they would come back the next day to volunteer, they were taken at their word. And then they would be held accountable.

Customers began to trust the community and started opening up during their visits. Sometimes they'd share they lived in the neighborhood or they were an artist. Each time they came in, the connection deepened. Asking questions about their art or their most recent home improvement project was an opening to more meaningful relationships. In turn, they would ask questions of us. It was important to honor and connect with as many people as possible in rich and deep ways. We tried very hard to do this with every customer, whether they had a home to do improvements on or they slept in the park.

Libby was working alone on a Saturday afternoon when a customer she recognized as a regular walked in. Carrie reintroduced herself to Libby, ordered lunch and went to eat on the patio. Friends came and sat with her, but as they left, Carrie remained on the patio. Close to closing time, Carrie came up to the counter. Libby asked if she needed anything else and noticed she had tears in her eyes. Libby rushed around the counter to hug her and began crying, too. Libby is an emotional and empathetic person—when someone cries in her presence, she usually cries too. When the two were able to stop the tears, Libby asked, "Why are we crying?"

Carrie shared with Libby she was able to contribute generously to the box that day for the first time in a long while. She stayed all day because she wanted to see all the different people her donation helped. She had recently found a better paying job and was no longer underemployed. She wanted to share her good fortune with others like it had been shared with her on so many occasions at SAME. She explained to Libby how she appreciated the dignity and delicious food she received and how she felt valued when she came in. It was quite different from the vulnerability that other experiences had created in her life.

Carrie returned many Saturday afternoons to dine and donate. She wanted to make sure many others had that same experience and enjoyed good, healthy food. One Saturday, she introduced us to a guy we had seen with her on a few occasions. From that Saturday on, they ate lunch together. It wasn't long before the two of them announced they were getting married and asked us to cater their wedding. We were beyond honored they wanted to include SAME Café on their big day, so of course we accepted. Libby even got to make their wedding cake.

Sometimes these conversations took place in the dining room, sometimes at the front counter, and sometimes when working together in the kitchen. It made people feel valued to know they weren't invisible. People who feel valued and like they belong somewhere will protect that space, resource or relationship.

The relationships we encountered through the café were what kept us going back day after day. The people, the conversations, the connections—all of those fueled us. Every one of those encounters taught us something, and we learned so much. We grew as individuals. The community surrounding SAME Café did as much for us as for anyone.

Darin first came into our lives during the summer of 2013. It was during a period he had been sleeping in the park just a couple blocks away from the café. If he couldn't find a safe place in the park, he would sneak into a building nearby and sleep in the laundry room.

One day he heard about SAME while he was hanging out at another nearby non-profit. He wasn't sure SAME Café was real or not, or if it was some type of scam, but he decided to go check it out. He was intrigued to find that it wasn't a handout—he could work off the food and that meant a lot to him.

In Darin's own words: *"Not only was the food good, but you guys always, always smiled when I walked in and didn't give me that look of pity or disgust — 'Oh no, there's that guy again.' Something about that opportunity to work made me feel good . . . It made me feel comfortable—feel human. It felt like being surrounded by family . . . helping gave me a sense of purpose for at least an hour a day. And then when I ate, I was proud because I had earned that food. It wasn't just something that was given. And I hadn't earned anything in a long time."*

When I asked Darin what brought him back, he shared the following: *"You looked me in the eyes* and it was like you knew what was going on with me, and you didn't care. It felt like you gave a shit about me when most people didn't. Eventually I got it into my head that this wasn't how I wanted to live. You were treating me so well, and yet I kept doing those things to myself. I could come in and if I had some sort of accomplishment, I felt like I could share it with you and the staff and everyone was so happy for me, it gave me the strength to actually go home to my parents to share those things.

"You were like my family and that was what I needed. I loved that Libby would put me on dishes, because it was really hard but it was something I was good at, and it felt like I was needed. It isn't so much the fact that I didn't have money, it was the loneliness. It's like every man for himself out there, and I spent a lot of time bitterly alone with nothing to look forward to until I found SAME—then I had something to look forward to in my day.

"Being able to share my accomplishments really helped my recovery process. And you let me put my volunteer work on my resume, and that helped me to get work because it showed that I had desire to work, that I had been doing more than just using for the last five years. I would go to an AA meeting, then volunteer at SAME, then back to AA, then home."

Darin eventually saw a flyer for a foundation on the bulletin board at SAME that offered financial help going back to school. He applied and was accepted into the program. With that organization's help, he finished school with a degree in video production and was able to find a job on a local film crew.

Darin still comes in to SAME from time to time and is proud to share with the new staff about his time there. Years after we left SAME, we got an email from Darin updating us on his journey and his success. Recently he started his own non-profit organization to help artists who are in recovery. He had been given an award for his outstanding achievements, which included the ability to gift $1,000 to an organization of his choice. We were honored that he chose SAME Café to receive this gift.

Before the café opened, Libby and I had allowed ourselves to become somewhat isolated. Many of our connections were with people we worked with or people with which we had prior relationships. We did little to expand our sense of community. Our country had shifted to focus so much on the needs of the individual rather than those of the greater whole. Being at SAME Café over the years allowed us to experience a sense of camaraderie and connectedness we didn't even realize we were missing until we felt it. The circle of connections around SAME included hundreds of volunteers and thousands of customers, many of whom we would come to call friends.

Not long after getting my tattoo, I was showing it off to someone in the kitchen while working at the front counter. The gentleman I was serving asked if he could do his volunteer service later. He wasn't having the greatest of days and needed to get to a meeting. By this point, I knew when someone said they need to go to a meeting it usually meant Alcoholics Anonymous or Narcotics Anonymous. There was a location for meetings not that far from SAME Café.

He was a good-looking man who appeared to be in his late thirties but was clearly at a low point in his life. He hadn't showered in a while and his clothes were a bit grimy, but he was trying. I could see the pain in his eyes. He seemed embarrassed to be asking for help but appreciative. I told him it was no problem, but after he ate lunch, he decided to stick around and help anyway.

He came back a few times and I learned his name was Sean. He was a good worker, following through on tasks, diligently doing the jobs assigned to him. He said please and thank you a lot, which was rare, and I wondered how he got to SAME.

On another day later that week, I was working in the basement trying to get some bills paid and Sean asked to "holler at me." I made my way upstairs again and there he was waiting. He led me out the front door onto the patio and I got a little nervous. Usually, "Can I talk to you outside?" doesn't mean good things.

Once we were outside of other customers' earshot, Sean said the first day he came to SAME was the lowest day of his twenty-seven years on the planet. I realized just then how hard life on the streets must be for this young man. I mistook him for someone at least ten years older. This was his first experience with homelessness, and he was miserable. He was truly hungry for the first time in his life, and he was scared.

Sean shared how amazing he thought SAME Café was and wanted to say how thankful he was for the space. I began to tear up. I hugged him and told him how much we appreciated his hard work. He walked away silently. As I watched his back disappear down the sidewalk, I thought to myself how I was truly grateful for this space for so many reasons.

That day, I was grateful for Sean for continuing to show me people are people no matter how they are struggling, and we all struggle sometimes. I saw something in him that reminded me of a lot of our regular volunteers and customers, like Gary, Carrie, Bud and many more. We all have hopes and dreams and want to be treated with dignity. We all want to be needed, and we crave connection. SAME Café gave all of us a sense of belonging. Being able to be connected at SAME provided everyone the chance to not only survive, but to thrive.

In February of 2014, SAME Café passed yet another milestone by serving the 100,000th customer. Mulberries Cake Shop brought over a beautifully decorated cake to help celebrate the occasion. All the staff and volunteers on hand that day anxiously waited as we watched the tally for the day increase. Who would it be? Would it be a first-time customer or one of the regulars? As soon as the lucky person came to the counter, we all threw confetti in the air and shouted out, "Congratulations!" Mulberries even made an individual cake she was able to take home as a prize for helping us break the 100,000 barrier.

It wasn't so much the number itself that mattered. More significantly was the fact that SAME Café had far surpassed the bar that had been set to measure whether or not it was a success. That was no longer a question. Within that number of 100,000 customers served was an unknown but certainly significant number of meals served that made a difference. It may have only made a difference for that person on that particular day. Nonetheless, a difference was made. That unmeasurable impact was cause for celebration.

It was important to celebrate those victories as they came along. Each milestone passed was validation that SAME was doing something good and was on the right track. Also, taking opportunities to celebrate the positives made it easier to weather the times that weren't so great.

Bud was covered from head to toe in ink, and he probably intimidated most people. I was definitely intimidated the first time he came to the counter to order lunch. Mandy was bashful and quiet, also ink covered. This couple would come into SAME Café nearly every day. They almost always sat at a tall table against the wall. He was the first tattoo artist I had ever encountered. I was impressed with his creativity and ingenuity with a needle. The two would meet up at SAME on Bud's lunch breaks. Sometimes Mandy would come in by herself and work on art projects. All their artwork was a statement of personal identity whether it was on their bodies or on paper. Sometimes, the couple would disappear for a while, but eventually show back up again. We were always excited to see them return.

I remember during one of those absences, I was super worried about them because it had been a long time since we had last seen them. When they showed up this time their physical characteristics had changed drastically. They did not look well. We never talked about the reason for their time away. After a few months of being back at SAME, they began to look like themselves again, no longer gaunt and exhausted. They shared they had moved into a new place and had even planted a vegetable garden.

Bud now worked at a new tattoo shop on Broadway. When I shared with him that I was thinking of getting a tattoo, he got excited. He became more animated as I described my idea. I got the inspiration from the story of the Long Spoon I had heard years before.

> A man dreams he has met God and asks to be shown the difference between Heaven and Hell. God takes the man to a long hallway that has two doors opposite one another.
>
> He opens one door and the dreamer sees a long banquet table full of piping hot, delicious food, but all the faces around the table are gaunt and in agony. They have arms that don't bend at the elbows and are holding long spoons; thus, they cannot get any of

the delicious food into their mouths. Seeing the starving anguished faces, the dreamer says he has seen enough and asks to see Heaven. God takes him back into the hallway and closes the door.

They cross the hall together and open the opposite door. To the dreamer's surprise it is a very similar scene, except this time the faces around the table are happy and satiated. While observing the long banquet table set exactly as the other room, he realizes these folks are happy because they are using the spoons to feed each other.

After hearing this story at some event and having the experiences of SAME Café, I knew I wanted a long spoon tattoo and I knew I wanted Bud to do it. His face lit up when I asked him if he'd be the artist. We talked design and I showed him pictures of work I liked, and he began to plan. He invited me down to the shop on a Friday night. I don't know if I have ever been so nervous.

Upon arrival, he had artwork ready for me to approve. I immediately fell in love with his design. He made some minor adjustments as he placed the transparent paper on my arm, and then began a five-hour tattoo sitting. Libby sat on the sidelines and watched as Bud created his magic. It was a long process but not as painful as I

—

thought it would be. When it was finally complete, I was so proud to show it off and love telling the story whenever people ask about it.

Chapter 14

It Wasn't All Fun and Games

The café's location on Colfax Avenue certainly brought us our fair share of tough customers. A lot of people who found themselves living on the street battled with drug and alcohol addiction. Libby often would say, "If I had to sleep in the park, I might drink myself to sleep too." When would-be customers came in drunk, they were often times angry and aggressive, which wasn't conducive to building community. Deescalating a situation with someone who was being unreasonable because they were under the influence was never easy. SAME Café staff tried very hard to never involve the police. Even the best-intentioned police officers don't always listen to vulnerable people and often don't have the tools to help. People who are dealing with mental illness or drug and alcohol issues do not need more trauma in their lives. Our experience with law enforcement was many times they escalated situations to a more dramatic level than necessary. We focused our efforts with difficult customers on de-escalation. Sometimes that was easier than others. Libby admits that

—

she was not very good at this. Her emotions run high, and she felt protective of the café and the people in it. Aussie John called her Mama Bear sometimes, and he even brought her a Mothers' Day card one year.

Early on, customers could stay and eat lunch even if they were inebriated because we thought it would help if they had something to eat. However, after many hard situations, it became clear that wasn't productive. When some people are intoxicated, it is difficult for their bodies to be in any space in a safe way. An intoxicated customer can't build community, might struggle to hold hot food, fall asleep in their plate, start fights or ask other customers for money. We wanted SAME to be a space for everyone. When you are a single mom bringing your children in for lunch, it doesn't feel safe to have a drunk person spill their hot soup on you or your children.

The practice was established of giving inebriated customers food to go and asking them to come back on a better day. This tactic wasn't always well received. There were times the food we offered was thrown back over the counter in anger along with some harsh words. Other times, the food was dumped on the sidewalk just around the corner. But as long as we stayed consistent and held everyone to the same standard, it felt like the right thing to do.

Up until this point, Amber was a regular customer. I had seen her enough times to know her name and I also knew she was struggling. Unfortunately for all of us, she started to run with the wrong crowd. One day when Libby was working by herself, Amber and her new boyfriend came into SAME Café totally lit—high on something crazy—not any behavior Libby recognized. We had seen our fair share of people struggling with alcoholism or meth addictions, but this was different. She describes them as being unbelievably out of it. Neither one recognized she was not going to serve them. As Libby tried to ease them out the door, they were not having it. They both began to get irate and started loudly calling her names. Strangers and friends got up from their tables and moved closer to the action. A couple of regular customers in the café came to Libby's side.

The situation got so intense Libby thought she might need the cops for her safety and for all the customers present. She can clearly remember Amber telling her boyfriend to "Take that bitch out." As soon as she said it, Libby describes the world as moving in slow motion. She saw his hand in a fist heading for her face. The thought crossed her mind she was going to know what it felt like to get punched in the face by a man. Fear ran through her, and at the very last second, she was able to dodge his right hook. She has no idea how, but is sure it had more to do with his level of sobriety than her boxing skills. Customers rushed in to protect her and pushed him and Amber out the door.

After the initial shock of it all, she hurried and locked the door. The two challenging customers stayed right outside, banging on the glass, throwing chairs and tables at the windows. Their aggression seemed to escalate with every minute that passed. As she looked around at the frightened people inside the café, Libby realized she had to call 911. It seemed to take forever for the cops to arrive. When Libby called me to tell what happened, she said, "I don't know if I have ever been more scared."

The couple took off when the squad car finally pulled up. Customers and volunteers alike rehashed the story to each other and the police. Eventually, the day returned to normal after many hugs and reassuring conversations. Kathleen, our neighbor at the cake shop, even came to check on everything after she noticed the commotion. Libby remembers feeling so shaken but reassured by all the love and support. Most of the customers checked in with her before they left to make sure she felt safe. Some who had never volunteered before even offered to stick around and help her close.

That's the amazing part of community. Although there can be challenging days and situations, there were many more times when we were genuinely awed by people. As frightening as that situation was, it brought people together for the common cause of ensuring neither Libby nor the café were hurt during the incident. Even people who were relatively new to SAME were drawn to the café in new and stronger ways. Libby felt the value of community that day in a way she had (thankfully) never experienced before.

I began to take a step back from the day to day operations. I was overwhelmed by the amount of suffering I saw each day. I was struggling to have hope and to find joy in the work. I was certainly not taking care of myself the way that is necessary to do this kind of emotionally demanding work. Libby took on the burden of doing my job in addition to hers and plowed right through, which was probably not the healthiest way to deal with this either. I continued to see people connecting and appreciating SAME Café, but it was like a fog fell over me in the space. We were making a living but not making a life. My joy in building community was challenged by all the hardships we had seen.

Ryan North once said, "Our brains are wired for connection, but trauma rewires them for protection." We saw a lot of folks who had experienced trauma and were struggling to be able to maintain a healthy outlook. After a lot of reading and research, I learned what I was experiencing is known as secondary trauma—indirect exposure to trauma through exposure to people who have been traumatized themselves. I wasn't focusing on the great things happening every day. I was not able to find hope. I was having trouble keeping my anger from becoming meanness and my sadness and disappointment from collapsing into despair. I was losing track of something I know in my core; that all of this was for the belief that deep down, people were good. And being good to one another matters.

The following quote from Anne Frank hits the nail on the head:

> "It's really a wonder that I haven't dropped all my ideals because they seemed so absurd and impossible to carry out. Yet I keep them because, in spite of everything, I still believe that people are really good at heart."

Zack was the kind of person that thought SAME Café was perfect. He'd come in almost every day of his life after sleeping in an abandoned house or a park. On his good days, he was sober and willing to help out. He was appreciative of the opportunity to eat a good meal and chat with people. He was super friendly and interested in the lives of those around him. Other days, he was the opposite. He was high as a kite or drunk as a skunk and struggled to even hold a coherent conversation. We'd hand him a cup of soup and ask him to come back another time.

On his good days, he was a hard worker—focused and diligent. He and Libby would have in-depth conversations about life and books. He was an insatiable reader. He would read anything Libby suggested—often sharing books from the free library in the dining room. He learned to love reading while in prison.

Zack had a hard time finding and keeping a job due to his extensive record and struggles with drugs and alcohol. He worked in construction doing day labor most days. He'd be out on a job and performing well. The site boss would see his work ethic and hire him again. Sadly, as soon as Zack accumulated any amount of money, he'd spend it on drugs and alcohol and would usually find himself in jail. This cycle happened repeatedly in the years he came around. As soon as he'd get out of jail, he'd beeline it over to SAME Café and start it all over again. Saying this time it'd be different because he was sober and really wanted to try.

In these sober moments, he'd share his hopes and dreams with us. He once told me he wanted to start a food cart downtown where he'd serve soup out of edible bread bowls. He wouldn't need much money to start it. Once he even had a lead on a cart, but not long after that he landed in jail again. He'd write from jail saying how sad he was that he wasn't able to be in his daughter's life and how he wanted to turn his life around.

There were several times we helped Zack buy things he needed, like an alarm clock so he could get up and go to work in the morning. Never wanting to give him cash, we would walk to the Salvation Army Thrift Store or RadioShack and get what he needed. He would eventually pay us back. Libby even went to court once for one of his custody battles.

At one point in his sober-ish cycle, he met a couple who offered to help him buy tools so he could do construction work on his own. They believed in him and his potential, as we did. They wrote up a contract and spent about $1,000 on tools. Zack would come in on Saturdays and keep us posted on his progress and tell us about the jobs he was doing. We were so proud of him. He was saving money and completing jobs. The night before his first payment was due, Zack disappeared and so did the tools. Shortly after that, we got another letter from jail. Zack had gotten into trouble again, claiming someone jumped him and stole the tools and his money. Who knows what actually happened, but we had to wonder if alcohol and drugs had something to do with it.

Later we got a call from Zack letting us know he was out of jail again. He was doing good and working at a job site where the boss was allowing him to sleep at night. But he was cold and uncomfortable and needed a sleeping pad and blanket. I said we could loan him a sleeping pad and blanket of ours. He was appreciative and agreed to meet up after the café closed. We decided to meet at a downtown restaurant at 6:30 pm.

At 5:00 pm Libby got a call from Zack on her cell phone. Immediately she knew something was off. Zack was slurring his words and asking where and when they were supposed to meet. Libby calmly said she was not going to meet him after all since he'd been drinking. This brought on an onslaught of insults and yelling. Libby hung up. Zack called back repeatedly and continued to scream at her so we turned off our phones. Then he started to call the café and leave terrible messages. When we arrived to work the next day, there were seventeen nasty messages from Zack, who "had not been drinking."   He claimed he didn't understand why we wouldn't help him. He tried to come by the café a couple of days later— totally inebriated. Once again, we asked him to come back on a better day. After much shouting he left, still upset that we wouldn't help him.

A few days later I answered the phone to hear Zack's voice. He seemed sober enough and I thought he was calling to apologize for his inappropriate behavior. Instead of an apology, he asked me for money. I lost it. I couldn't understand this person and his inability to see why I was so frustrated with him.

Speaking with Libby about it, I was bewildered and hurt. Neither of us could find any solace. We both were disappointed, angry and felt an overwhelming sadness when it came to Zack. It seemed we wanted more for him than he wanted for himself. He had so much potential but could never quite get his shit together.

When Libby sat down with him one day, she tried to reach him one last time. She explained why we were so sad for him. She reminded him he doesn't get to spend time with his daughter because of his challenges with sobriety, but even that didn't seem to phase him. He thought his life was perfect. He insisted he didn't need to change, but that we should accept him and his alcoholism.

It was clear to us he would never overcome his tendency to self-sabotage unless he wanted help. We could not force him to hear a message he was not ready to receive, but at least we planted the seed. His biggest battle was the one he was fighting with himself. He mattered to others but just not to himself yet. We cared about him more than he cared about himself. And yet we still have hope for him.

I hope one day he will get the help he needs, see his true potential, and be the good dad that he wants to be. I hope there will be mental health services available to him when he is ready to receive them. I hope society starts to take better care of each other.

Chapter 15

Time to Transition

Over time we noticed the neighborhood around the café was changing drastically. The thrift store down the street had closed and the space turned into two separate, fast-casual restaurants. Next door to SAME, the dress shop shut down and was replaced by a high-end hair salon. What had once been a 24-hour diner on the corner soon became a hipster bar and taco joint. Café customers began to move out of the neighborhood due to rising rents and had to travel farther to get to SAME.

Lisa was a regular at SAME and often brought members of her family to dine with her. She loved the food and the atmosphere, often hanging art on the walls of the dining room. Her art was amazing and we loved to support her in this way. She usually walked or drove over to the café when it was raining.

Lisa was a "starving artist," and as rents rose in the neighborhood, she could no longer afford to live close to the café. She moved a few blocks farther out, but when funds again ran short, she was evicted from that apartment as well. She lived in her car for a while, parking close to the café so she could have easy access. When her car was eventually booted and then towed, she found herself homeless.

Thankfully, more stable housing became available for Lisa, but it was much farther away from SAME Café. She had to take three buses to get there from across town. Those three bus rides meant she had to leave hours before she wanted to eat in order to get to SAME Café before closing time. It also meant every part of her existence thus far had to change. It was more effort to find housing, food and places to share her art. Even just getting her paintings to the café to hang meant an all-day ordeal for her. If you ever tried to get a large package onto a bus, you might understand just a bit of her daily struggle. Essentially, experiencing poverty was Lisa's full-time job.

The board had long been thinking about a food truck and how to reach folks outside of our brick-and-mortar facility. We were very excited about the prospect of reaching more people and taking SAME out to different neighborhoods. At one point an intern worked tirelessly to conduct a point-in-time survey. Armed with the results of that survey, they developed a business plan and feasibility study for the truck. We and the board spent months talking about it and sharing the idea with people.

The food truck idea certainly had traction, but nonetheless the idea stalled. Libby and I would fall into bed at night exhausted from the long day and talk about what was next for SAME. When we thought about the food truck, a new excitement would roll over us. But then we would try to walk through all the things we had to do in the next couple of days and forget all about the food truck.

We'd bring the idea up at each board meeting with the intention of getting somewhere. But we were so spent from running the café we had very little energy left to dedicate to planning another program. As much as we wanted the food truck to happen and knew this was a potential next step for SAME, we knew we were at the limits of our working capacity. Libby worried about managing two programs with two budgets, multiple employees, and how a food truck would utilize volunteers. I worried about all the details—getting a license, finding a truck, who would run it, where to park it, and where to buy it? Then there was the question of how do you build community on a food truck? How would people be able to volunteer with that kind of setup? After many months of thinking and talking and worrying, we came to realize Libby and I didn't have the bandwidth to make it happen.

During this same time, we found ourselves reaching out to a local non-profit expert for mentorship. As the co-founder of several successful non-profits, our mentor was someone who could walk alongside us and guide us through some of the challenges of a changing and growing organization. She could also offer us advice on a personal level. She made sure we started to take care of ourselves. It was awesome to talk to someone who had started and worked for many non-profits and understood the challenges. She also suggested we read a book called *Non-profit Lifecycles: Stage Based Wisdom for Non-profit Capacity* by Susan Kenny Stevens.

This book became a tool for us when later we found we were at a significant turning point as an organization. So All May Eat, Inc. had grown beyond the start-up stage and was ready to enter the stage of growth. Growth is necessary to ensure a non-profit's survival beyond the point where many similar organizations stall out. Those often suffer from "Founders Syndrome," which can steer an organization into stagnation. It was becoming clear to us that we, as the founders, were possibly the cause of blocking opportunities for entering the growth stage.

As Libby's sister Katie pointed out, we certainly could have learned how to run a non-profit with multiple programs. We learned how to open and successfully run a non-profit café. And she was right, we could learn. But after reading the non-profit life cycles book and learning more about Founder's Syndrome, we started to contemplate what we really wanted for SAME Café. We wanted SAME to continue to grow and be around for years to come, but I was struggling to see how to make that happen.

At this point, I was stretched so thin. I was even more exhausted from the daily struggles. I was disappointed I didn't have the energy or the strength to do it all. I knew people were still connecting and building community at SAME, but I could not see the forest for the trees. I couldn't see good things were happening every day. I was so stuck. The anger and disappointment I felt weighed on my heart daily. I was mad that the world dealt people like Zack such a shitty hand and that society just continued like nothing was wrong. I started working less and less in the café, unable to find any way to recharge my spirit.

All this stress played into the daily interactions with the staff as well as the customers and volunteers. We had been so lucky over the years to have so many wonderful and patient employees who cared immensely about building community and treating everyone with dignity. However, we could feel the frayed nerves and uncertainty that we were feeling about the future of the café spilling out and affecting those relationships.

I felt it was time to step away from running the café, but Libby still wasn't ready. She kept steaming ahead and continued to push through. It was much more difficult for her to let go. This was her way of making all that was wrong in the world right. Her motivation each day came from the starfish story. Originally credited to Loren Eiseley, this story tells the importance of making a difference in small but powerful ways.

One day an old man was walking along the shore. As he looked down the beach, he saw a human figure moving like a dancer. He smiled to himself to think of someone who would dance to the day. So he began to walk faster to catch up. As he got closer, he saw it was a young man and the young man wasn't dancing, but instead he was reaching down to the shore, picking up something and very gently throwing it into the ocean.

As he got closer, he called out, "Good morning! What are you doing?" The young man paused, looked up and replied "Throwing starfish into the ocean."

"I guess I should have asked why are you throwing starfish into the ocean."

"The sun is up and the tide is going out. And if I don't throw them in, they'll die."

"But young man, don't you realize there are miles and miles of beach and starfish all along it. You can't possibly make a difference!"

The young man listened politely. Then bent down, picked up another starfish and threw it into the sea, past the breaking waves. "It made a difference for that one!"

After one very stressful week before one of the biggest fundraisers of the year, it finally became very clear to Libby we needed to step down. She had an intense response to a minor mistake made by an employee. The pressure had gotten to Libby and she just lost it. That interaction made it click for her that it was all too much. As much as she loved being in the café and building community with people, she realized we were holding SAME back from growing. We had been burning the candle at both ends for too long, and we no longer had the energy to give that the community deserved. It was time to find someone else to begin operating SAME Café or we were going to have to shut it down. Either way, we personally needed to be done.

We were finally on the same page, even though it was heartbreaking and neither of us really wanted to be there. It seemed like an admission of failure we weren't able to do it all. For weeks, we had tough conversations with each other about what needed to happen. We also had no idea what life beyond SAME Café would look like for either of us. What would people think if we stepped down? Would we look like quitters? What about the people we had been serving for years—the people that counted on us and felt like our family? Would they feel like we were abandoning them? These weren't easy questions for us to ask each other or to hear. Our identity was wrapped up in this community and how could we exist without it and vise-versa?

After weeks of exhausting deliberation, we finally came to a decision. At our next board meeting, through many tears, we shared it was time for us to step down.

Looking back, we could and probably should have done things differently. We never should have let it go for so long before raising the white flag. We could have hired on help sooner, and we could have delegated more of the tasks of the daily grind. But the control freak in Libby has a motto— "Delegation leads to disappointment." We often laugh about how she has a hard time letting go. We should have taken more time away to rest, rejuvenate and refill our own energy supply. After all, you can't give to others from an empty cup. But at this point it was too late, and we had let it go on for too long.

This was not an easy time to be on the board of SAME Café. Founders leaving a non-profit can be really challenging. It was important to all of us that we moved through this process with care and focus. The board asked some experts for advice and spent many hours processing the complex next steps. At one point, the board discussed the options of merging with another non-profit or even ceasing operations all together. After much conversation, the general consensus was to continue and look for new leadership even though we had a hard time fathoming how to make that happen. Both Libby and I took a deep breath. We didn't want our decision to step down to the be the end of such a beautiful thing. At the same time, we were overwhelmed to think about how to find someone to do what we were willing to do every day. The board was committed to ensuring SAME Café would continue to live on beyond this monumental transition. We got great advice from our mentor about finding someone who was a good cultural fit for SAME, someone who could dig in and do some hard work but who also had the passion for the mission. We sent out an email to the community letting them know where we were at and where we wanted to go. It read:

> SAME Café is our passion and it has been amazing to watch it grow. Brad and I have been in the restaurant almost every day for the last 10 years. We have scrubbed toilets, taken out 1,000 of pounds of compost, made over 175,000 cookies. We have built lasting friendships over the dish station and have watched lives be transformed by this community of healthy food. This has been the most amazing and challenging 10 years of our lives.
>
> People often ask us how we do it and sometimes, we even wonder how. Our heart and passion are

this place and we want to see it here for many more years to come.

We are excited to share that we are ready for a transition in our lives. We are hoping to separate ourselves from the daily operations and really start thinking about SAME Café and the bigger picture. This is our time to step back from the day to day, and with some distance, define new roles for ourselves. Over the course of the next year, we will be hiring several new employees to take on the day-to-day operations. We will ensure that every function previously performed will now shift to our new employees.

We are excited to lead and not to manage. This is the most critical juncture in SAME Café's growth and development. And we want to bring you along in this process. We are so excited to search for and find people who can continue our creation. The success of this transition is in finding strong people who believe in healthy food access and dignity and who have experience in program directing and growing organizations. This is such an exciting time for SAME Café.

We and the board have been thoughtfully preparing for this transition for a while now and will continue to do so. You can follow along on this journey here in our newsletter and on our Facebook page. The next couple of steps in the process will be seeking out staff that will stabilize the organization through this transition and setting up a transition committee to help with this process.

We promise to keep you updated on the progress of this transition. If you know someone who would be a beautiful addition to the SAME Café staff, please do not hesitate to send them our way.

This is not Brad and Libby saying good-bye. This is Brad and Libby trying to let go and see what is next for SAME Café. Cheers to the next step in this journey we call life.

We knew we had to find the right people to take over SAME. We needed people who believed in the philosophy as much as we did and could take care of our baby. To be honest, it was such a hard process. It felt like we were looking for needles in a haystack. Ultimately, it came down to finding people with the heart to love the mission and who had the skills to do our jobs.

What we have learned over the years is teaching people how to run the kitchen and non-profit is not the hardest part. Teaching people to walk alongside others and keep compassion at the forefront in the midst of the day-to-day challenges is almost impossible. It was even more challenging if they came to the interview thinking that they were applying for just another kitchen position. Working at SAME Café requires the desire to work for more than just a paycheck. It means building community at the same time as you are peeling carrots. It means asking questions about other people and listening to them authentically. It requires that you can be in the space and do your job while getting to know the customers and volunteers. Not only this, but you need to be able to set healthy boundaries and be vulnerable, to lead by example and meet people where they are. This is easier said than done. It requires a lot of intention, finesse, and effort. We found some people naturally gravitated towards positions like these. Other people spoke well in the interview about their interpersonal skills, but in the end, they didn't really have what it took.

It didn't help that Libby and I were wearing all the hats in the café, and that we wore them interchangeably. We had no idea how to write job descriptions for our roles. The board tasked us with writing down every job we did during a typical week, and then sorting those together into logical groups. In doing this, it came to our attention we would actually have to hire three to four people to be the leadership team. We had no idea who would be willing to jump into one of those positions and take on all that responsibility for very little pay.

Because I had already stepped back and Libby had taken on quite a few of my responsibilities, the board decided to work on replacing me first. That way those tasks could be taken off of Libby's shoulders once the new person came on board to be the operations director.

Shortly after publishing the job description, we got a resume from Letisha (Tish). She had tons of experience including working at Whole Foods, a local farm-to-table café and a local vegan hotspot. All the places she recently worked spoke highly of her and we were impressed by each of the connections. We had even eaten at the farm-to-table restaurant where she had been a chef because they had hosted many community events. Several awesome volunteers came from that vegan restaurant where she had been a lead baker. She had also volunteered with another food focused non-profit in Denver with which we worked closely. We felt the universe brought her to us and we are so grateful.

While Tish had to learn how to manage volunteers and not do all the food prep herself, it was clear she had the heart and passion for the mission. We stressed how important it was to honor the volunteers, keeping in mind it didn't matter how the onions were chopped. It mattered that the person chopping the onions was valued and included. I was able to work directly alongside of her for almost seven months, training her and helping her learn the crazy way we do things before the kitchen became totally hers. Once she took the reins, it was amazing to walk in the café and taste the delicious food Tish had made. Libby loved how clean she kept the kitchen. We knew we had made a good choice.

After all the talk about finding new leadership for SAME, the universe seemed to be answering our call. First it had brought us Tish, and a few months later we seemed to be getting closer to finding an executive director who really understood SAME Café. It was overwhelming to read the piles of resumes that came in once the position was finally posted. We conducted multiple rounds of interviews with potential candidates. Many of them were more than qualified for the role. Surprisingly though, not one of them had been in the café before. Then, I was elated to see a familiar name in the pile.

We had known Brad Reubendale as a customer and a volunteer. He first came to SAME Café after losing his job as a pastor for coming out as gay. He loved the access to healthy food and appreciated how the anonymous payment system preserved his dignity. When Brad got back on his feet, he found a job at a youth shelter not too far from SAME. He became manager of a job readiness program and would bring teens from the shelter to volunteer in the kitchen at SAME Café once a month. The young people worked on developing job skills for a few hours and then they would stay to have lunch. After getting his graduate certificate in non-profit management from Colorado University, Brad had taken a job in a development role. When he heard about the executive director opening at SAME Café, he realized he was ready for a new challenge.

After a lot of deliberation, the board boiled it down to the top two candidates, one of which was Brad.

We understood Brad had never been an executive director, but we knew he had the heart we were looking for in a leader. Not only that, but he understood the café from both sides of the counter. When we spoke on the phone for his initial interview, he was more concerned about what was happening with Libby and I than the details of the job.

After having him come in to spend some time in the kitchen to see how he interacted with staff, volunteers and guests, we had him sit down with the board of directors so they could make the final decision. After all, they were the ones he would be reporting to if he was hired. Not surprisingly, the board voted to hire him unanimously.

Brad had gone from needing SAME Café to sharing it with others, and eventually, to leading it. We could not have found a better fit. We affectionately started calling him Brad 2.0. Libby and Brad 2.0 both like to say, "We were unicorns looking for another unicorn." We were so lucky we found him.

During his onboarding process, Brad 2.0 started asking some deep questions about SAME and why we operated the way we had for so long. He started visiting other community cafés in Colorado and would come back full of questions. A lot of these conversations were challenging for us. This was really intense work. We were trying to translate the essence of SAME and "because we know it's the right thing to do" was not enough of an answer. He really wanted to understand how we came to each conclusion. We credit him for his mindfulness and persistence here because he really wanted to live and breathe the mission like we do. The only way to do that was through these probing conversations, no matter how painful they were for us sometimes.

I remember one such conversation in the tiny, dark office in the basement. We were all crammed in under the florescent lights late one night after the day was done and Brad 2.0 asked us why SAME Café did not have a suggested donation. This particular question struck a nerve for Libby right away. Her reaction was a little heated. This was the first time Libby felt like she might have to fight for SAME Café's identity. I understood right away Brad 2.0 wanted to know why so he could defend it. Libby wanted to make sure he knew he could not change it. That was something non-negotiable about SAME.

We explained we knew firsthand how awkward it could be standing in front of a cashier wishing the suggested price was different. We had been to other events where suggested donations were "expected" and knew we wouldn't be able to meet the suggested donation. It never felt good because to us, "suggested price" meant "minimum price." It always felt alienating, and we felt less than. Our goal was no customer at SAME Café would ever experience that feeling. Again, it goes back to the conversation about everyone having something to give. We shared with Brad 2.0 we thought building community was not easy when you start by making someone feel less than. He agreed 100%. Having been on the other side of the counter, he knew how that felt too.

That was just one of the many deep conversations we had with Brad 2.0 about the essence of SAME and what was non-negotiable. He listened with love, respect, and an open mind. He would push us sometimes to elaborate and explain some things in more detail. We spent hours in conversation. The more time we spent together, the more confident we grew in his ability to lead SAME Café. Libby and I still were not sure how to step back and let go. Thankfully, we were able to get some help making that decision.

As we were transitioning to Brad 2.0, SAME Café was awarded a chance to participate in an intensive training with an amazing organization called Uncharted. After being selected as one of very few organizations who would get to participate in this event, we realized just how lucky we were. Uncharted put Brad 2.0, Libby and me in touch with mentors in various fields who were able to see our strengths and challenges and guide us through this transition process. We made relationships with mentors and experts who still help us today. Those folks brought to our attention that SAME could and would be successful without us at the helm because of the strong foundation we were able to lay. We just needed to trust our new leadership team and get out of the way.

This was really hard for us to swallow. At first, Libby and I wanted to remain board members even after the transition ended. Selfishly, we thought we'd need to stay in the loop somehow. Although we were exhausted, neither one of us could imagine SAME Café operating without us. We thought it would always need us and no one else could provide for this community the way we did. As we moved through the process, doing more research with each step, we learned founders serving on a board after leaving is not healthy for an organization. Often times, people refer back to the founders instead of to the new leadership when decisions need to be made or when things get challenging. Essentially, it is clipping the wings of the person who is now in charge. After lots of soul searching and conversations with our mentors, we decided we needed to eventually step all the way back. We would give Brad 2.0, Tish and the board of directors complete autonomy to drive the organization to new heights.

Part of that stepping back included actually leaving the area for a while. We knew if we stayed in Denver, we would smother Brad 2.0 and Tish. Knowing ourselves, we would be in the restaurant daily, or at least weekly, checking in on our baby. To everyone else, this would mean overstepping our bounds. We needed to trust the team that was in place. In theory, this shouldn't be a problem, since we selected them because we knew they had the skillset to do the work. They just needed a chance to build relationships, change things around, and make space for themselves in this community without us looking over their shoulders every second. The only way that was going to happen was if we literally left town.

Chapter 16

Our last official day of work was October 6, 2017. During that week, lots of friends and family stopped in to have lunch and say good-bye. One person even brought Libby a necklace that had been given to her mother for her lifetime of service to community. Libby was so honored to be gifted such a special memento. On Friday, Brad 2.0 and Tish had arranged for an open house style party after the café closed. As a great surprise to us, Libby's mom even flew out from Illinois to be there.

Those few hours were a whirlwind of smiles, hugs and happy tears as we visited with wonderful people who had become such a huge part of our lives over the past decade. It was almost like a wedding reception where we did our best to make the rounds to visit with everyone. Of course, there was an adorable cake from Mulberries. Someone read a proclamation from the Governor of Colorado who had declared October 6, 2017 to be Brad and Libby Birky Day. We both cried our eyes out.

That final day was a walk down memory lane. Many volunteers from the early years made the effort to be there. So many familiar faces were present. It was overwhelming. What it brought to the forefront of our minds was SAME Café was not about Libby and me. Although this celebration focused on us, every one of those people who sent a message, came to eat cake, or hug us that day had been a part of the success of SAME Café. It was a celebration of community and investment in each other. It was a passing of the torch.

For over a decade we had been so busy. We constantly lived by our Google calendar. Each day we would wake up and go from picking up vegetables to the café to countless meetings and/or events related to SAME. Seldom did we ever have the luxury of wondering what we were going to do from one day to the next. Being bored was never a problem we had to worry about. My sister liked to tease Libby that she didn't know how to sit still. She thrived on making a to-do list and checking items off.

With the baton now handed off to the new management team, that phase of our lives was coming to a close. The reality of letting go and not being an integral part of the SAME Café operations was finally starting to sink in. Who were we without the café to define us? What were we supposed to do from day to day? How could or would we continue to build community?

It was with all those questions (and more) in our heads and very few answers that we put SAME Café and Denver into our review mirror. For a long time, we had been wanting to take a trip to visit community cafés in other parts of the country, and that fall seemed like the perfect time to do it. We packed up some clothes and our two little dogs, hitched our teardrop camper to the back of the car and started to drive.

The trip was a victory lap of sorts. We were able to reconnect with people we had spoken with and mentored over the years. So many community cafés had opened around the country, and we finally had the opportunity to visit quite a few of them. Every café we visited and each person we met with was an affirmation that all the blood, sweat and tears we had experienced since 2006 was beyond worth it.

While we were on the road, we spent a lot of time reflecting on the previous twelve years. We would often dig up a memory or story we had previously forgotten— one that made us laugh or cry or possibly a bit of both. Thankfully, Libby had the good sense to make some notes about those memories before they faded away once again. The stories and interactions that occurred during our tenure at SAME Café had a deep and profound effect on us. It seemed important to save those stories and somehow make them publicly available, knowing it was possible they could have the same effect on other people as they had on us.

When the idea of SAME Café came to us, it was just that, an idea. It began like a single drop of rain. Each additional drop pestered us until the downpour of possibilities was too torrential to ignore. If we had ignored it, I would probably be managing some IT department. My days would consist of sitting in front of a computer, bored beyond belief, mindlessly searching for the end of the internet. Libby would be beginning her twenty-fifth year of teaching elementary students, lamenting about how terrible parents are these days.

It was thrilling when that first customer came in who wasn't personally connected to us. When thousands of others continue to come in who are not Libby's sister's co-workers, my friends from the office, or some family from Libby's classroom, we are amazed and giddy. In some ways, we breathe a sigh of relief that it actually works. In other ways we are elated and quietly chant in our heads, "I told you so. I told you so. I, I, I told you so!" (That's a *Scrubs* reference for anyone who is curious.) Any time we see SAME Café in the news, one of us will softly elbow the other and whisper, "We did that!" The delight never seems to fade.

Taking care of people through food made us happy. People came in because they wanted to be there and appreciated all of it. I love that this idea resonates with everyone. We aren't the only ones who felt SAME was needed.

We are not foolish enough to think places like SAME Café can change everything that frustrates us about the world. But we do know SAME Café and the people we met there were a shelter for us during the storms. This book had to be written because what happened at SAME and what continues to happen there every single day matters. People matter. Our connections to each other matter.

People were invested in the space and the magic that happened there. Many of those people would never have come to know each other in any other way if not for SAME. This café made space for people to be there for each other. Not just to feed each other but to nourish each other. We were positive the nourishment would continue long after we left.

The people we met along the way taught us to be better, constantly reminding us how to be human, to be present and to listen. Through this café, and others like it, people are accepted and in turn, accept others. Total strangers connect through sharing a meal and become friends.

"Through food you find out there is more that connects us than separates us."

—*Dr Jessica Harris in High on the Hog*

We are all slices of a larger community. Each one of us is beautiful and amazing on our own. However, when we are given the opportunity to join together, we become stronger. Only then does the bigger picture, the one that matters to all of us, come into focus. People change each other and touch each other's souls.

The entire experience was challenging at times, but the stories of hope and love are the rudders that keep us moving in the right direction.

—

Who knows where life will lead us next? Whatever we do and wherever we go, we will keep these relationships with us and continue to hope, be present, and act with love.

Acknowledgments

First and foremost, I am grateful to my wife, Libby for her trust, her love and her strength as we journeyed along the path that led us to SAME Café and beyond. Her contributions to this book were invaluable. Without her support, this book would still be a few pages of unreadable gibberish sitting on a flash drive collecting dust in my desk drawer.

Thanks to every volunteer who cut vegetables alongside us in that kitchen and to every customer, whether you ate at SAME Café once or you were a regular. Without you there would be no stories here to tell.

To our friends and family members who spent innumerable hours helping us get SAME Café off the ground and to keep it going all those years, especially our parents for believing in us as we took the road less traveled, we are eternally grateful for your love and support.

To the infamous Brad 2.0 and the Denver team, every one of you have played a part in ensuring our baby not only survived the transition but continues to thrive. Brad, you are forever our unicorn, and we will always be grateful for your leadership. We are so proud you are continuing to feed the fire that started out as a tiny ember in our brains that just wouldn't be extinguished.

To authors Adrian "SoulFoodScholar" Miller, Shawn "Extra Mile" Anderson, and Nate Ragolia, thank you for taking the time to encourage an aspiring writer, while at the same time warning just how much work it takes to complete a book.

Thank you just isn't a strong enough sentiment to send out to the incredible Mary Thomas for reading, rereading and holding us accountable early on to the writing.

Much gratitude goes out to our wonderful friends Cindy and Bonnie for their encouragement and for letting us know what was missing.

Thanks also to Susan Newton for your amazing feedback, professional experience and excellent notes on version 521 of this book (I think we might be on version 643 by now).

There is no way we could tell all the stories we witnessed and held in our hearts during our time at SAME. There were countless volunteers, board members, donors, customers and sundry other characters who shaped our lives and taught us so much. We are so grateful for the conversations that enlightened, entertained and emboldened us to keep going on the days that weren't so easy.

The idea for SAME Café came from a collection of experiences volunteering during the most formative years of our lives. We both took trips with our youth groups where we learned the value of working alongside people. Those experiences shaped our souls and made us who we are today.

Much appreciation for the people who taught us to cook and to appreciate food—Grandma Birky, our moms, culinary school instructors Chef Hagen and Chef Lamb from MSU Denver.

Thanks to the numerous people who hosted us and our van as we drove around the country trying to clear our heads and remember the magic.

This wasn't meant to be a book. We just wanted to not forget the stories. In writing the stories down and sharing them with people, we realized it mattered that they were shared. We are thankful to say there is no end to this story. True communities never end—they just evolve. We can't wait to see what comes next!

About the Author

Brad Birky is a social entrepreneur who is currently calling Florida his home because it is the warmest place he could find; also there are dolphins. Brad and his wife Libby co-founded SAME Café and now consult with non-profits around the country on best practices. He is an avid runner and outdoor enthusiast who is a voracious reader and researcher. He loves to cook for his wife and take his dogs, Leo and Gemini, on long walks.

CPSIA information can be obtained
at www.ICGtesting.com
Printed in the USA
JSHW011935051222
34380JS00001B/9